AF579838

The Power of Defeat

Not a guide to IIT JEE

Prof.Karanam Bhanumurthy

Former Visiting Professor
Department of Metallurgical Engineering and Materials Science
Indian Institute of Technology Bombay (IITB)
&
Former, Head Scientific Information Division
Bhabha Atomic Research Centre
Mumbai
India

INDIA · SINGAPORE · MALAYSIA

Copyright © Prof.Karanam Bhanumurthy 2023
All Rights Reserved.

ISBN 979-8-89133-889-0

This book has been published with all efforts taken to make the material error-free after the consent of the author. However, the author and the publisher do not assume and hereby disclaim any liability to any party for any loss, damage, or disruption caused by errors or omissions, whether such errors or omissions result from negligence, accident, or any other cause.

While every effort has been made to avoid any mistake or omission, this publication is being sold on the condition and understanding that neither the author nor the publishers or printers would be liable in any manner to any person by reason of any mistake or omission in this publication or for any action taken or omitted to be taken or advice rendered or accepted on the basis of this work. For any defect in printing or binding the publishers will be liable only to replace the defective copy by another copy of this work then available.

Disclaimer

1. This is a work of fiction. Names, characters, businesses, events and incidents are the products of the author's imagination. Any resemblance to actual persons, living or dead, or actual events is purely coincidental.

2. The opinion expressed by the author in this book is his point of view and has nothing to do with the Institutes mentioned in this fiction or the Indian Institute of Technology Bombay, (IITB) and Research Centre (Bhabha Atomic Research Centre) where the author worked earlier.

Dedicated to

Students and parents

To all those students, who follow their own path towards excellence.

To all those parents, who allow their children to realise their own dreams.

To all those teachers, who make students realise their potential.

Finally, to my parents, who accepted me as I am and also made me fit enough to live the way I wanted to be, not always "successful" but "meaningful"

"The front cover designed by Prof. G.V. Sreekumar, IDC School of Design, Indian Institute of Technology, Powai, Mumbai. 400 076. India"

About the front cover

The natural process of fading (drying) of any leave is from outer side to inner side. Here, the leaf is drying from inside (connected to the stem side) to outer side leaving the rest of leaf ahead quite green.

This symbolizes, that the defeat has originated with in you and the only way forward is to accept defeat , analyse and do appropriate course correction towards success.

Contents

Acknowledgements

(It is my wish that all readers to have a glace of this section)

To be honest, I never believed in myself and never felt the need to write this novel. Several events and incidents have forced me to take this difficult journey, and after I decided to write, I faced several constraints to complete it. In addition, as this is meant for young students, I always had self-doubt about whether I could convey what I wanted to. Finally, I completed it, as I strongly believed in the basic concept of this project. I must admit that I could not have done this alone.

I would like to acknowledge the large number of students who have contributed immensely by sharing their life journeys. At times, apart from sharing their successes, students have shared their failures. The motivation for writing this story is to compile their successes and failures and make their thoughts alive through the characters depicted in this novel. I am grateful to all students, and without their support, this novel would not exist.

In the beginning, I narrated the contents to students, teachers, and some of my friends. I have received feedback indicating that the theme of this story is highly relevant to students appearing for difficult and highly competitive examinations (IITJEE, NEET, JAM, etc.), and all attempts should be made to provide a gripping and highly motivational story using characters that are true and that many students could easily identify with. It was also suggested to provide a few broad guidelines on the criteria that may need to be exercised by serious students before taking on such a hard journey. I am fully aware that students themselves are the best to make their decisions; however, some guidelines are given, and to be honest, they are not exhaustive.

A large number of students in this generation are easily distracted by social media and addicted to worthless entertainment. In addition, they often use logic to disregard cultural values and ethics. The purity of thoughts and mind plays an important role in any success, and this aspect is emphasized without the use of any religious texts or sermons. I want to acknowledge all of my teachers who have shaped my understanding, especially on spiritual matters. The readers may feel at places that there is some deviation from the real story and at other places long conversions that may appear not to be related to the theme of this novel. As a student and also as a teacher, I suggest the readers, especially students, read these chapters where I have stressed the importance of self-help as the best help and that intervention from higher powers for positive benefits is always there to come.

I would like to sincerely thank all of my friends and colleagues at the Metallurgical Engineering and Materials Science Department at IITB, especially Profs. Viswanathan, Narasimhan, Dinakar, and Vinay. They have contributed immensely to this novel. I would like to especially thank Prof. Sreekumar, Industrial Design Center, IITB, for designing the front and back covers of this novel.

I would like to thank my friends at the Materials Group and Knowledge Management Group at Bhabha Atomic Research Centre, where I have worked for more than three decades. I would like to especially acknowledge the support I had received from Venu, Amarendra and Viswanadham with whom I had close associations for more than four decades.

I would like to especially thank Dr. N. Ramamoorthy, who has been a constant source of inspiration to complete this novel.

I cannot express enough gratitude to Mrs. Jayanti Murthy and Mr. Murthy, who have participated in various discussions and provided several editorial corrections. I am ever thankful to them. I would like to thank Mr. Devarajan who has helped me at various stages of this novel.

I would like to especially thank my morning walking friends, Subhash, Surriender, Krishna, Manish, Sunil, Rajendra, Sanjay, and Paramanand, who always added strength to my arguments. There were exchanges of wisdom, innocence, ignorance, and intelligence, all of which have added value to this novel. The morning walks are the bright spots of any given day. I am thankful to all.

I would like to acknowledge my publishing manager, Rasika R and editor, Dainty W from Notion Press, for their outstanding contributions.

I would like to express my gratitude to both brothers Murthy and Ravi and their families, who have always listened to me patiently and to my crazy decisions and loved me no matter what I am.

I would like to especially thank Aditya, my son, who is a unique, generous young adult with so much passion. This book would not have been possible without him, and he is the real motivation and constant source of energy to complete this book.

I would like to thank my late wife, Sudha, who always encouraged me to do what I liked, and I am sure she is somewhere up there wishing me the best. I would like to say that whatever I have achieved is due to the selfless service of my mother, Shakuntala. To my father, who never questioned me and let me do what I wanted.

Finally, I would like to acknowledge the community of students who are responsible and engaged in this work, and I am inspired by many of them to overcome my defeats and make my life meaningful.

Preface

How does the mind work?

Most of the time the operating system of our brain, the mind, may not give the right feedback to act correctly during extreme stress or failures.

The only way forward is to fix your eyes and ears on experienced people with wisdom with rapt attention without any prejudgments.

I am not a writer, nor did I want this novel. There was never a strong compulsion to write a book. I always considered myself a good storyteller but never a good writer. I made most of my learning in a vernacular medium, and hence there was never a need to write long stories or share my experiences in English languages. However, I had an inherent talent to read a novel and appreciate the author's mind and their commitment to writing and expressing their thoughts coherently. Based on my experience, I am of the opinion that writing is not my cup of tea, and I convinced myself that I do not have the necessary talent nor a desire to tell a story.

All this changed that night.

After that particular incident, which I am going to describe to you all soon, I was convinced that language is only to express thoughts, not to generate thought processes. What is needed for an expression is a thought, an experience, a commitment, and a strong will to communicate to the readers and thereby experience a sense of satisfaction. At the same time, you get a feeling that not knowing quality English should not be an impediment to expressing yourself. I know I have lived with this criticism and accepted this as my limitation. It is for the reader to appreciate or criticise my work. I am here only to tell the story that I like, and I would like to leave the judgements to the readers.

Then why did I write this book? I have seen several students and parents going through a difficult thought process. It was a big surprise to me that not many bother to share their sorrow, limitations, downsides, and failures. Most of the time, many shared only success stories, and many did not feel comfortable sharing their failures. I am a living witness who collected the information and also tried my best to be part of their journey, to a very select few, who shared their experiences. I have been a reservoir to collect these experiences, assimilate their journey, and share my little understanding for the benefit of others. I am also like many ordinary men, but one incident that night, which I had witnessed changed all this. I have taken all the courage to narrate the story in all its reality. I know my shortcomings and do hope readers will excuse me and appreciate my efforts.

It was a pleasant evening at Kota, Rajasthan railway station. There was some breeze and respite from the hot sun. I am a regular visitor to Kota to inspect nuclear reactors, and this has been part of my official duty. I am a nuclear scientist by profession, which automatically makes me think logically and rationally. I have compared myself with others during several discussions, and I could easily convince others based on facts. I am not forcing readers to believe me but trying to convince them that this story is written by a scientist, who is an above-average logical thinker, and I am sure this will motivate readers to read this story with more intensity.

Again, let us come back to the story, not a story, it is reality, an incident that forced me to write this book. I was tired and eagerly waiting for the Rajdhani train to come. I was on my way back to Mumbai. A train was expected at 10.20 pm. I had a confirmed second AC ticket. I am lucky that I am a government servant, and the government allows me to travel by second AC for an official visit. However, for my personal travels, taking into account the payment package, I can only travel by second-class sleeper coach. Second-class AC by Rajdhani has a distinct advantage, as it provides good-quality food along with soup. I was only thinking of good food and sound sleep after exhaustive work.

All this changed that night.

The train came at platform no. 5 and was late by about 20 minutes, a fair punctuality, by Indian railway standards. I entered my carriage, and mine was a lower berth. I could adjust my luggage and felt that all three berths were empty. The train pulled out and was picking up speed. Just then, a middle-aged Maharashtrian couple entered the compartment. How silly of me; I should have seen the reservation chart. They were accompanied by their daughter, who was maybe 18 to 20 years old. All three looked very gloomy and filled with grief as if they had lost a near and dear one. The girls' eyes were swollen, and so were their mother's. The father's eyes were moist and seemed to be in control of his emotions. After seeing the couple, I lost interest in the food and the soup, which I had dreamt of all along. I just went out and asked the T.C. if I could change my seat. My intention was only to provide the Maharashtrian family more privacy and, above all, more freedom to be on their own. I was not keen to understand their problem as I knew for sure that I could not solve it.

Destiny leads to a place of its choice and is mostly not liked by you. The T.C. said the second AC was full and looked at me curiously as if I was demanding something extraordinary. His expression confirmed that I was illogical and just troubling him to change my berth unnecessarily. He said with authority that berths were not available and that I was lucky to have a confirmed berth. I just thanked him profusely and came back to my berth.

By then, the Maharashtrian family had adjusted their luggage, a big aluminium trunk of massive dimension. It could not fit under the seat but was protruding out, making it difficult to walk out of the coupe. I had decided to keep quiet and not request them to rearrange the aluminium trunk, as I was not going to spend my entire life on this train journey. Generally, there is a fight among most travellers on matters of trivial importance, and Indian railways are notorious for this. Now we know most of the people who travel by the Indian railways belong to my category, as they do not want to pick any quarrels and during the process to suffer.

I started looking out of the window. It was dark, and one could hardly see anything except the dim and flickering lights at a distance. As the train picked up speed, the melancholic atmosphere in my bogie peaked. It is important to describe that young girl, her mother called her Snehal. Snehal had beautiful eyes and a near-oval face. Her long, thick, black hair had a parting towards the right and combed back and appeared to me very beautiful. A few of her hair strands were falling on her forehead, and Snehal was just pushing them back with her hands.

There was life in her face, and practically, she would have given a good fight for a good role in any of the Hindi movies if she had worked under a good director. I thought she would have made a wonderful actor. She was not dressed well, and she was fairly tall, close to 5 feet 4 inches, and had a very healthy body. If she was looking so beautiful on her worst day, you can imagine how beautiful she could be if she dressed well. I could see tears rolling down her cheeks, and she was wiping them with her maroon dupatta. The handkerchief was already soaked and was beyond use. Sometimes her mother was consoling her, and she was herself beyond control, weeping profusely. The atmosphere was tense. We generally avoid weeping in public. Now, I was sure that the reason for the sorrow was something that I could not imagine. I just kept quiet, I also started feeling sick, having an induction effect, and remembering my unhappy days. Everyone passes through ups and downs, and that is life. The atmosphere just sparked off my thought processes and remained in the background all along.

Just then the caterer came for the night dinner. The family said no. I was also so immersed in my own thoughts. I had no option and also said no. Here it is important to mention, that sorrow or joy is just like an induction, and it changes the atmosphere, even if you are travelling with people who are unknown. This happens only in India.

Just then Snehal's mother said, "Bhaisaab, you please take food." I had to lie to her that I was not hungry. They did not press further. The caterer looked amused and went out. Now, I plucked up all the courage I could muster and asked Snehal's father about the reason for their unhappiness. I have travelled extensively in India and abroad, and I am sure these informal inquiries about co-passengers happen only in India. We are taught to share sorrow and happiness, and the more you share, the magnitude of sorrow comes down, and the magnitude of happiness increases. This, I realised every time I returned from abroad. No matter from which state, no matter from which caste, no matter how rich you are, there is something called the inherent Sanskar Culture built in every Indian to initiate a talk and share their sorrow. This you realise only if you go abroad, where the formal sharing of anxiety-sorrow does not exist.

Again, I asked Snehal's mother, "Bahanjee, you are so upset, I know I have no right to ask for the reason, could you please share the reason for your sorrow? It is often said the intensity of the sorrow comes down to sharing with others." There was again a big silence. I just kept quiet. It was around 11:30 p.m., and I thought I should not press further. I just went out to walk in the corridor. I must admit that I was not insulted as my repeated attempts to get an answer for their sorrow failed. Snehal must have thought and realised that and came out along with me. She just called me Sir, I was very happy, she did not call me Uncle. Maybe I looked younger than my age or she felt that she should not become close and kept aloof. She just came to me and started to cry again. I cannot explain my feelings. It was definitely not pleasant, and most of the time silence kills. I just touched her softly and consoled her, trying to initiate a conversation with the intention of reducing Snehal's burden of sorrow. I had no feelings. I did not know Snehal. She just came to me for solace or to pick up the conversation. There is no name I can attach to this relationship. It is just friendship, maybe a sense of being together, and above all, it is the sharing of human emotion.

She just looked up and came closer and said, "Vishnu Sir, please help me." I could see her presence of mind, as she had seen my age and name at Kota and was willing to enter into conversation with me, on one condition that I should not disturb her parents. I could understand and promised Snehal that I would never broach the topics in front of her parents.

Snehal started narrating her story - it has happened to Snehal and it will continue to happen. I am just reproducing below what Snehal had told me with all the grief in her mind. I tried to narrate in my own style but stuck to what Snehal had narrated to me that night.

Snehal and Ravindra are siblings and are very close. Their parents are working; their mother is a primary school teacher, and their father is a sub-inspector near Pune. Most Indian parents expect their children should excel. I have yet to come across any parent who does not wish success and progress for their children, especially in studies. Snehal is senior to her brother by two years. They were doing well in their studies, and their performance was exceptionally good, and their success was much ahead of their classmates.

When Snehal was studying in class 10, there was a neighbouring boy by the name of Mihir, he had passed IIT JEE and he had studied in Kota for coaching. Local teachers felt Snehal was better compared to Mihir at the 10th level, and they should admit Snehal at Kota for the required guidance. The teacher had no hesitation that Snehal would clear IIT JEE. This would totally shape her career. Snehal also dreamt as if she had passed the exam, and she had no reason to disbelieve her teacher.

Now, the problem is that Snehal is a girl, and living in Kota is difficult. It was also difficult to avoid going to Kota and continue their studies in Pune. The parents also do not have much finances to send Sneha to Kota and have two establishments, one at Kota and another at Pune. Moreover, Ravindra, Snehal's brother, was in the 8th standard, and his education also had to be taken into account before the final decision was taken. Imagine what sacrifices an Indian parent can make. Also, imagine the pressure the parents unknowingly place on their children.

Mrs. Godbole, Snehal's mother, resigned from her teaching job, sold their small house near Pune, and moved to Kota. This forced Mr. Godbole to move into a rented house in the same locality. This was not appreciated by most of the neighbours. This decision to sell the house, resign a job, and establish a family at a relatively unknown place like Kota, especially for a girl child's education, looks insane. Most of their friends and relatives thought that this was foolish and that they were making a mistake, which they would repent later. In addition, most of the neighbours thought their action was just to belittle them. No one came to see them off at the railway station when the Godbole family left Pune. It was with this background that the Godbole family left Pune to find their future in Kota.

Now, anyone can imagine the risk taken by the Godbole's family, whether it was a good or a bad decision, only time will tell.

Snehal continued to narrate further, and there was extreme shrillness in her voice. As I understand from the softness of her voice, she must also be a good singer. The Godbole's family arrived at Kota established their family and started acquainting themselves with a new dimension in their life. They were convinced that they had made the best decision of their life. As no one knew them in Kota, nor their financial background, there was no pressure on them to continue to stay at Kota except for the financial burden, which was always there for them to reconcile. They admitted Ravindra to class 9 in a well-known ICL school near Vigyannagar and also admitted Snehal to class 11 without much difficulty.

The next big thing was to get both of them admitted to the best coaching classes. They have been correctly advised by their teacher in Pune and Mihir's parents for all the right guidance. As we know, successful parents show the right way for others to follow, so they don't go through the same pain and sorrow that they had endured. No one tells the hard facts, but everyone will narrate the good side only and sugarcoat the bad aspects. No one will understand the difficulty and facts until you yourself experience it in Kota.

It was the month of May, and Kota was scorching hot. Godbole's family had seen hot summers in Pune, but Kota's weather was unbelievably hot. In addition, the ashes thrown out of the thermal power plant made life even tougher. They endured all the difficulties for a better tomorrow. The family lived in Kota against all odds, facing testing times, and Snehal's father used to visit them once a month to comfort and reassure them that they were on the right path.

Two years passed, and Snehal moved slowly from 11th to 12th and tried her best to perform well at various stages of internal examinations and also performed well compared to her friends. In the meantime, Ravindra had completed the 9th standard, wrote the 10th exam, and things moved fast for the family. Financial problems combined with health problems, tension, and the anxiety of uncertain success at the examination were always a worry for them. This has always been a source of concern for all the family problems, and more so for Snehal.

Finally, the results of IIT JEE were out, and the result showed that Snehal had not qualified. All the hard work and health issues resulted in nothing except "the loss of two years."

Now, the problem was that Ravindra had been admitted in class 11, and they had paid the fees in the coaching classes. Ravindra also wanted to go through the same cycle as that of Snehal, and no one wanted to go back to Pune. Snehal was in a state of shock, despair, frustration, and, above all, the ignominy of not clearing. On the other hand, most of her friends cleared IIT JEE and were looking forward to happily joining IIT.

Here, the pains start. The intensity of pain and sorrow cannot be explained but only experienced. In normal terms, failure and success are two sides of the same coin, and one should not be affected so intensely. It was the decision to leave Pune with high expectations and a huge financial burden that had compounded their problems.

At times, when the situations become beyond control, it is recommended to change the place, at least temporarily to bring solace leading to calmness in the mind to make a rational decision. It is at this point they were planning to go to Solapur to visit Snehal's aunt's place. Now, the reader can imagine the cause of their sorrow, it was an uncertain future for which Snehal was not mentally prepared.

Snehal felt helpless, lost her confidence, and had no one to look forward to for solace, as both parents were upset. Sometimes, Snehal also felt that she had caused considerable pain to her parents, and this added to her anxiety. The misery of parents due to children is quite enormous and not expressed is also not understood by teenagers. Snehal felt more pain when some of her friends cleared these exams, and this feeling made her more insecure and more uncertain. She felt that her life was doomed and as a sister, she had not set a good example for her brother.

Most readers who have not experienced a situation like this may not be concerned and may come to the conclusion that Snehal's sorrows were normal and should not lead to so much frustration. However, all human beings are not the same, and Snehal was different. Above all, Snehal had never seen tears in her father's eyes. She felt that her father had to maintain two establishments and also discharge his duties in the office with all integrity. This added to Snehal's agony much more. She was also concerned about the reaction of her aunt in Solapur. The thought process of Snehal was weakening and driving her to hell.

At times, the pressure and tension are much, and many teenagers are not in a position to handle it.

It was at that time that Snehal was trying to open the door of the fast-moving train. It was around 1:00 a.m., and hot air was blowing into the compartment. Snehal was completely drenched with sweat and started moving slowly towards the door. I was so lost in my thoughts and concerned about Snehal's future. I never knew that Snehal opened the door of the compartment and she was moving slowly to the edge of the door, preparing to jump, and she was not even aware of her existence.

It was at that time that I realised something drastic was going to happen. I don't precisely recall what I did at that moment. I just rushed and forcefully took Snehal with both my hands and hugged her intensely. She was just shivering and totally drained from top to bottom. I cannot just explain those few moments of the past, and I do not know how long Snehal and I remained in the affectionate hug.

I just then realised, about the moving train in the presence of the child in my arms. Holding her in one hand, I closed the main door and touched her hair very softly. I started holding her close to me and started moving slowly to my compartment. Seeing both of us, her parents were worried and dumbstruck. Snehal had almost regained her consciousness and showed the essence of gratitude through her eyes. Eyes express everything, that we cannot describe in words. I also acknowledged with my eyes. Her parents could not understand our silent conversations, through eye contact.

I started to feel the intensity of the air conditioner, thanks to the railway department for keeping the compartment sufficiently cool, in spite of the external temperature being more than 40 degrees centigrade.

I did not feel like going back in time, particularly due to what had happened a few minutes back. I also did not warn Snehal's parents about the incident which made me profusely sad. I decided to take everyone along with me and make the present more comfortable so that the journey ahead became positive and bearable.

Now it was my turn to open my past, not so much to the past, but the recent past, and try my best to change the thought process that is going on in the mind of Snehal and her parents.

The story I had narrated to them was real and just happened a couple of years ago.

As I was narrating, Snehal sat close to me and was looking closely into my eyes. The parents were also listening with rapt attention.

No one slept that night.

I narrated this story through the eyes of Vishnu. As the story was at its peak, I could see the confidence level of all, including Snehal, was soaring.

The story is so real; many may easily connect with it, and it is happening to several parents and their young children, testing their endurance limits. Snehal may be fortunate, but there are several students who are not so lucky. I wanted to reach out to several boys and girls through this story and reassure them that success and failure are two sides of the same coin and may not matter in the long run.

This story provides you with hope to handle extreme adversities and prepares you for the worst.

Everyone now recognises the importance and significance of IITs. This aspect is extensively discussed in both electronic and print media. My intentions here are not to add more information that is already available on the websites of coaching institutions but to look at each student and their parents from a human perspective.

My intentions here are not to overemphasise the success stories of IIT JEE-clearing students nor to underestimate the importance of coaching classes. My intention here is only to narrate a story I witnessed about the struggles of parents and children during the formative period of their IIT JEE preparation. This story is close to my heart. I would have never expressed it in the form of a book until I met Snehal. I was convinced that to reduce the extent of agony and frustration the students go through, I should work hard and tell the story in the simplest language, so that any student studying in their 10th standard can read, understand, and appreciate this. I am confident that this story serves its purpose.

On average, about 10 to 12 lakh students appear for the IIT JEE with the intention of gaining admission to the prestigious 23 IITs of national importance. Less than 2% of students who attempt to join IIT clear this exam. In comparison, on average, about 10% of students get admitted to the best schools in the US. This highlights the level of competition involved in clearing this examination. It is important to understand that coaching classes, in the name of imparting knowledge, assure parents and students about the success rate of their students. It need not be overemphasised that most coaching classes make substantial financial gains and profits based on contributions, mostly from unsuccessful students. These so-called coaching institutes again promise and stress how more than a large percentage of students clear the IIT JEE examination on their second attempt.

There are three levels of intellectual students. The first kind is the gifted students who achieve good ranks through natural study. These students pass and maintain their ranks in any examination, with or without coaching, and with or without family support. I do not intend to address these student or students in this novel. The ranks in between could be for the rest of the students who are attempting the IIT JEE for the second time, these students (second kind) may not be that gifted, but they have the necessary confidence and intelligence to give their best. Their ranks mostly depend on their presence of mind on the day of the exam, their level of confidence on the day, and their efficiency of performance in the given time. It is to these parents or children who are not so fortunate but still have the ambition to perform well in this exam in a credible manner that this story is dedicated.

There is another set of students (third kind) who see only a moon in the sky, forget about the beauty of the stars, and keep on working hard to get the moon. They are fully aware that they may not get what they wish, but somehow they do not accept their weakness and continue to work. There is a need to exercise caution and enjoy the beauty of the stars, and in fact, they are much better than the moon. One has to fine-tune one's demands depending on capability and adapt to them quickly.

Passing the IIT JEE is not the end but only the beginning. There are students who have obtained engineering degrees from other than the prestigious institution mentioned above but have fared better than the IITians, but in the process of preparing for this examination or, for that matter, any other examination, there is sufficient competition and challenge.

It was with these reassuring words that I started to tell the story to Snehal and her parents. The story that I narrated to them was so emotionally draining and, at the same time, sufficiently encouraging that it might have prompted them to return to Kota. In fact, it is important to mention that immediately after the completion of this story, the train arrived at Mumbai Central. Snehal and her parents got down at Mumbai Central and booked their tickets back to Kota. This is the strength of a few individuals who can be motivated, and their thoughts can be strengthened to take on the challenges of life.

It was around 7:30 a.m. The train arrived at Mumbai Central. I came back to reality. As it was a working day, I had to rush back to my residence and join duty. Otherwise, taking leave during the official trip is generally not permitted. I just got off the train and wished them the best. For a moment, I had eye contact with Snehal and could read more than what was going on in her mind.

Chapter I

The Defeat

Sharing failures

Everyone wishes to share only their success stories.

No one mentions their defeats and failures.

It is hard, rather very hard to accept failures and to understand that problems exist. Only those who accept defeat with grace, analyse the reasons minutely and take the appropriate course of correction to realise "what the power of defeat means."

At the Kota Railway Station

It was possibly early in the morning when the train from Mumbai pulled into the Kota Railway station. Madhava and his father, Vishnu, just got down from the second AC. Both of them were totally lost, in particular, Madhava, who was always wondering if he had made the right decision to come to this distant town from Mumbai. He was not comfortable, as he was inconveniencing both his parents and spending money. This was the first time he would be staying alone.

As they move to the exit gate, there is a mad rush by autos to take them to Vignana Nagar. Both of them knew the guest house was nearby, and they could walk as every rupee counts. However, the heavy load of books forced them to take the auto and move towards the guest house, which took them just a few minutes, but they ended up paying Rs 100/.

Just as they got out of the auto, Madhava started thinking again about how this all started and just felt a bit heavy as he moved into the guest house and started going down memory lane.

Before finally settling at the guest house, Vishnu asked Madnav,

"Are you really interested in doing all this? Even if you are in two minds, both of us can return home. Loss of money and time is not an issue; willingness is more important as the road ahead is very tough."

Finally, Vishnu says, "I do not believe in any advice but like to say, as you will be staying alone, never be afraid to accept defeat; accept with grace, and this makes you feel comfortable when you taste success; it will never overburden you as you move along."

Madhava listens with absolute silence and now knows what this loaded statement by Vishnu, his father, means: silence speaks volumes, whereas words fail you.

Vishnu and His Family

"Laxmi!" Vishnu exclaimed loudly one morning around 6:30 a.m. after reading the local newspaper.

Vishnu believed that his loud voice must have woken up most of their neighbours. However, his sweet wife Laxmi was still in deep sleep.

"Laxmi!" Vishnu called out even louder.

She opened her eyes and asked Vishnu what the matter was.

"Do you know, Laxmi, Manu Nair, who resides on the fourteenth floor of our building, has passed the IIT JEE and is ranked 249 in the IIT Advanced?" Vishnu shared with excitement.

Laxmi was not overly impressed.

"Alright, we'll congratulate him in the evening," Laxmi replied.

"Laxmi, this is not the 12th standard examination, and Manu has passed the IIT JEE with a good rank." Vishnu stated, his voice raised slightly.

"Well, I know this boy was working hard, and his parents were supporting him. That boy also got the 19th rank in the Maharashtra Board exam. What's the big deal about getting the 249th rank in ITI?" Laxmi responded.

"Laxmi, it's not ITI; it's IIT." Vishnu corrected her.

"Vishnu, how does it matter? A small change in the sequence of alphabets, ITI and IIT. Education is important; exams and ranks are not relevant." Laxmi remarked before returning to sleep.

So she said and she slept.

Madhav is the only son, and he is almost a duplicate of his mother in behaviour, action, and thought process. Madhav is not concerned about anything; his concern is for good food, quality sports, and especially cricket practices. By the way, he is studying in the 8th grade and practically has no interest in his studies. Vishnu's father was concerned about Madhav's future as he was not doing well in most of the examinations. The only face-saving is that he has a robust body and his continued passion for playing cricket. Lakshmi has inculcated Madhav with several good qualities, the most important being his visits to the temple with his mother every Saturday. This aspect was admired by all in our locality.

So, thinking about it, Vishnu just went back 15 years in time.

My parents wanted me to see a girl whenever I visited my native place. It appeared to me that the only ambition of my parents was to get me married and settle down as quickly as possible. They never inquired about my requirements or were concerned about the requirements of the girls. This time, my visit to my native place was practically after two years, and after reaching my place, I was immediately forced to go to Hosur, about 120 kilometres from my native place, to see this girl called "Shree Laxmi." That was the only girl I saw who said immediately yes and accepted her to be my life partner, not because she was quite good-looking; she was just a graduate, but because my liking was instantaneous due to her simplicity. In those days, all the villagers were involved in the process whenever the prospective groom visited the bride. This is no longer the practice. Finally, the conversation between Shree Laxmi and me, which took place about 15 years ago, should not be kept secret, no matter how irreverent this story may be.

"Vishnujee, I am a very straightforward girl. I have two younger sisters, and both of them are married. I also have an older brother, and he has waited a sufficiently long time and finally settled down happily in his life. By the way, my sister-in-law likes me, and they are all happy. To be honest, I am also happy in my present state, and the only unhappy people are my parents. My parents only wish to marry me to someone who can provide a simple but quality life for me and nothing more. Both my younger sisters are more educated, more beautiful, and more talkative than me. Because of this qualification, they could find their husbands, do well, and settle in the US. I am not that outspoken, and to tell you the truth, I tried my best to find someone so that I could also get married and relieve my parents of their burden. I was left behind, and both my younger sisters were already married. Who will marry me when my two sisters have kids? I have no regrets about my life." Shree Laxmi said. My only wish is to get married to someone who can assure a very simple life and wants to settle down in India. This helps me take care of my parents as and when they need it. I have no desire to even go to the US; forget about settling down in the US. My parents, who had been to the US, said that whenever there was a need for maternity and babysitting requirements, they travelled to the US only out of compulsion and always said their visit to the US was like a "Parrot in a Golden Cage."

"It is after a long time that someone like you from a big city like Bombay is coming to see me. Please be assured that if you marry me, I will be your good wife, like my sisters. Even if you don't like me, I will not feel bad, as many prospective grooms have rejected me for several reasons." Laxmi said.

As mentioned by Shree Laxmi, she is reasonably good-looking, speaks nonstop, and above all, has put in all the facts without any hesitation. This is the first time some girls have spoken to me so openly and expressed her views vividly. I did not think further, and I just said yes.

"Hi Vishnu, are you daydreaming?" Laxmi said it with a loud voice.

I came back to the present.

"Will it be possible for us to go and meet your friend, Mrs. Madhumita Ghosh?" Vishnu asked.

"Why are we remembering Mrs Madhumita, and that too in the morning, and that too by her first name? You always called her Mrs Ghosh." Laxmi said.

"Genuinely sorry. Please speak to her so that we can take Madhava to them and make him a little more interested in his studies." Vishnu says.

Vishnu, just reminded, Shree Laxmi that Ananaya Ghosh is the daughter of Mrs Madhumita Ghosh and Thimir Ghosh. She is well-built and not very fair; however, she wants to excel in her studies and please her parents in all her activities. Additionally, this couple is sending Ananaya for some good coaching, and she is also taking some examinations to improve her skills. With these thoughts in mind, Vishnu requested Shree Laxmi to fix an appointment with the Ghosh family so that Madhav's future could be better moulded.

"That is not a problem. We can do it on Sunday as both of the Ghosh family are working. They do not like gate-crashing, and I will try to fix an appointment for next Sunday, around 6:30 p.m." Laxmi said.

Actually speaking, Vishnu also personally liked the Ghosh family, and Lakshmi was quite aware of this fact.

"I am sure that they are not going to share any information that will help our sons for any future growth." Laxmi said.

Mr. Ghosh is from West Bengal and is married to Mrs. Madhumita, and both of them come from Midnapur, West Bengal. It appears that their marriage was a love marriage. Both of them are highly composed and speak very carefully, providing only the information you need. In other words, it was impossible to extract any useful information from this couple as they appeared to be highly reserved and introverted.

Their only objective in their life was to make Ananya unique and try their best to obtain information about various competitive examinations, excellent career guidance, coaching classes, and the best tutors for any consultations. They have acquired the necessary information related to Ananya's future, and they invested time and effort. They also expect others to invest time and hence do not feel comfortable providing information or, in their own words, with no spoon-feeding for parents.

Mr. Ghosh is a doctor by profession, and Mrs. Madhumita is a college teacher in Chemistry. Taking into consideration their busy schedules, it would be difficult to be friendly with them. Finally, it is difficult to find time with working couples as their schedules are tight.

On the other hand, our family is simple, with practically unlimited time and barely enough financial resources to make both ends meet. This simplicity makes life straightforward, as there are not many dreams to be realised. I never understood how their daughter, Ananya Ghosh, performed well both at school exams and various other competitive exams. This always kept me guessing why Madhav always performed so poorly.

Now my only dilemma was to prepare well and ask all the relevant questions related to Ananya and try to get relevant answers, especially regarding Madhav, as getting another appointment at another time was not easy. It was to the good grace of the Ghosh couple that they had agreed to meet us, all due to the simple and carefree attitude of Shree Laxmi. Lakshmi was entirely responsible for fixing this meeting, and I give her complete credit for arranging this appointment. The meeting was scheduled for 7:00 p.m. on Sunday. Myself and Shree Laxmi dressed well so that we could present ourselves better to the Ghosh family. To complicate things further, Madhav did not return from the cricket ground until 6:50 p.m. and finally arrived at 6:55 p.m. Madhav was fully bathed in sweat and said he was ready to go. I was aghast at his shabby appearance, and he may need at least an hour to make himself presentable before the Ghosh family. I am sure that we will not be able to make it at 7:00 pm as planned. Neither Shree Laxmi nor Madhava was bothered, and both of them took their own time as if this meeting was not their concern.

There was a phone call at exactly 7:05 p.m.

"Can I please speak to Mrs Shree Laxmi Vishnu?" Madhumita said.

"I am Vishnu speaking and will call my wife to speak to you. Ma'am, we are about to start, and I am in search of an auto." I said.

"Why a taxi or auto? It is only a few minutes' walk. Please come as quickly as possible, as we are planning to go out to Vashi to meet our friends." Madhumita said.

"I cannot understand the delay after fixing an appointment. Please remind Mrs. Shree Laxmi." Madhumita said again.

"No, ma'am, we will be there in no time. Please bear with us." I said.

Madhumita banged the phone with almost disgust.

I just hated myself for allowing this situation to occur. Madhumita and my dear son Madhav were making my life miserable. I thought I should have asserted myself on the phone, but it appears that I only dominate others in my dreams. I generally become so nervous and lose my presence of mind, and mostly I curse myself. Finally, we reached their family at 7:30 p.m. As soon as we reached their house, we exchanged pleasantries. I once again recollected all the things I should ask. The meeting lasted for about an hour and helped me open my eyes.

"So, Shree Laxmi, you wanted to discuss the possible exams and coaching classes for Madhav." says Madhumita.

In the meantime, their daughter Ananya came out, gave a pleasant smile, and inquired about our well-being. Madhav was not interested in any of this conversation and was asking Ananya to show him her video games. In the meantime, I compelled Madhav to wish the Ghosh family, and he did this activity with the utmost reluctance. I hated this, and I could do nothing. Just then, the Ghosh family asked Ananya to take Madhav inside and show him a video game.

"Ma'am, can you please inform us about the competitive examination and information related to coaching classes so that we can enrol Madhav for the same?" I said.

"I am surprised that all the information has been available on the school notice board, and the classes for advanced students have almost started three months ago. It is surprising to me that you have no knowledge about the competitive exam in standard 8th, and with this mindset, I am not sure how you are progressing." Madhumita says.

"You please inform us of the details, and yes, we have missed a few classes. It is also possible that we are not keeping track of what is written on the notice board." I very mildly reply to Mrs Madhumita.

I am surprised to see Mr. Ghosh; he is almost sitting silently and gives a feeling of not being interested in the conversation.

I can give you the phone numbers of the coaching classes and the information related to the QUEST exams and another competition exam. Finally, for more details, you have to check the school notice board. So saying, she handed over a piece of paper with all the details.

I understand that the information she has provided is quite adequate for the time being, and I have decided to check the school notice board more frequently so that Madhav's future can be improved.

"Amma, you just see, Ananya defeats me in all the video games, beats me in a car race, and boat race, and as I do not have any control over the jockey, I have no option but to lose the game." Madhava said.

For the first time, Mr. Ghosh interferes and requests that Ananaya teach Madhav control so that the game can be fair. Both of them go back, come back, and return after hours. I see a victorious smile on Madhav's face, and he says that he has beaten Aananya in all the games. I was surprised to know how quickly Madhava learned these video games, which Aanayan had been playing for more than six months. At that time, I thought Madhav was not a stupid boy, but given the right kind of environment and encouragement, he may excel, provided you allow him to get interested. At that stage, I profusely thanked the Ghosh couple and said that Ananaya was a sweet and very intelligent child.

It is important to mention the happiness of the parents when their children are appreciated. I could see a thousand-watt, bright smile on Madhumita's face. Finally, we left their place, thanking them profusely for all the help and advice. Madhav was in a playful mood and made a demand for video games so that he could better play video games and have an upper hand the next time he met Ananya. Neither Sri Laxmi nor Madhav showed any interest in the conversation. In addition, he was also planning to visit the Ghosh family next Sunday, as he was sure that the video games would not be purchased. Finally, Shree Laxmi stared at me as if nothing had happened. Looking at the school notice board is a waste of time, of no consequence, and no substitute for regular studies.

Finally, I must admit that certain people do not change.

The performance of Madhav was not impressive at X standard; however, he decided to pursue XII standard and proposed to take M, P, C, and electives as electronics and did not show any interest in taking biology as he hates dissection of animals as a practical during the zoology experiments. He had no interest in taking any coaching for entrance examinations, as he wanted to play cricket and be happy.

In one of the interschool cricket matches, Madhav realised that his performance was too bad, and above that, the level of cricket played even at the HSC level was so good that he had no chance of succeeding in cricket as a career option. This made Madhav realise that sports are a serious business, that playing cricket is important for health and for making friends, and that taking it as an option for a career is beyond the imagination. At that stage, he thinks that his father was right to take his studies a bit seriously, and it is not too late. He makes the decision that he should take his studies more seriously in order to succeed well later in his life. Madhav decided to meet his own Mr. Ankush Patel, and he has done his X exam very well. He has also passed the NTE and a few Olympiads. Everyone has to learn from mistakes to do better, and changes come at the right time and not by force.

Two years passed by slowly with all uncertainties and with no serious effort in studies and taking things lightly, and in the end, the performance at the XII state level exam was good, but the most disappointing was "Not Qualified" in the IITJEE exam." In spite of taking the best coaching classes and giving their best, at this stage, the real reasons for the failure were sinking in as they moved along, and it was too late to make any corrections.

Vishnu made necessary arrangements for Madhav to stay in an apartment in Kota to take IIT JEE exams for the second time and Madhav started feeling the pain of staying alone.

Apartment in Kota

"Idiot, have you shifted to this place recently? Understand to switch off the geyser and also close the running tap to preserve water. We all stay on limited water resources." Madhav shouted at Mahati.

This stunned Mahati and she was aghast, as no one, including her own parents, had been so harsh, especially when she had made no mistake.

What impressed Mahati was the innocent rebuke of Madhav; there was no cruelty, no bitterness. It was just about saving water and helping the owner take preemptive action. How can anyone say such things without even looking at the person, whether a boy or a girl, and yet be so firm?

As it happened, without a word, Mahati ran to the common bathrooms, closed the tap, and switched off the geyser. She was stunned by her own behaviour, just obeying the orders and feeling happy. Mahati had all the facilities in her room, and she was not responsible for any lapses there. Still, for reasons unknown to her, she felt the need to act against her own wishes.

No one knows why, at times, we listen with utmost seriousness to strangers because we believe they mean no harm to us and have the courage to speak up. This doesn't happen often but only a few times.

Mahati had just moved to Kota, in that apartment, that very morning, trying to adjust to the new circumstances against her parents' wishes. She had moved from an extremely luxurious apartment in Mumbai to a very ordinary place, and she was still trying to understand the reasons behind it.

We do many things against our own wishes, and this was one such step she was yet to convince herself of. No one knows what the future holds, as nothing moves along a straight line, just like in a war. Life, as you live it, is no less than a war and is always fought mentally with unknown adversities.

Try to be comfortable in those situations when you find yourself in extremely uncomfortable and unpleasant circumstances. Just follow and listen to your heart.

The Punjabi Doctor's Family

The Gambher's multispecialty hospital is situated in Bandra (west) and is close to a 100-bed hospital. This nursing home has all the facilities that any modern hospital needs, and possibly much more. In addition, the best doctors in Mumbai and in India are on consultation, and several doctors from abroad are always available on call. This nursing home has a reputation for treating the richest and providing solutions for any ailments. However, these facilities come at a very high cost. This hospital is mostly used by the elite class, and several cases that could not be treated were referred to this hospital. The most modern facilities are available, or they have an understanding with other hospitals to get the test done; in fact, these facilities are in working condition and are available round the clock. The resident doctors, the technical staff, the nurses, and other medical staff are in close contact and have excellent cooperation, and this was the key to getting the best treatment on a very urgent basis.

The success story of this hospital is not relevant to our story.

This hospital is owned by Dr. Ganbhir's family and essentially belongs to Harpreet Gambhir and Swarna Gambhir. Harpreet did his MD at leading medical colleges in Delhi and later moved to the USA to specialise in general medicine. He has been instrumental in modernising this hospital from scratch, and his wife, Dr. Swarna, also gave substantial support. Dr. Swarna comes from a very rich family, and there was a lot of support from their family, both financially and emotionally. Dr. Swarna is an MD in gynaecology, has a super speciality from the UK, and is an expert in this area. The infertility clinic is part of this hospital. In fact, due to the large financial investment, she has absolute control over the functioning of the hospital. She is the last word, and no one has any authority to overrule her. Even Dr. Harpreet is sometimes scared of Dr. Swarna, his wife, but never shows it to the staff. The couple could get along for the last 20 years due to the accommodating nature of Dr.

Harpreet. Their nature and their relationship are very important to our story.

The couple has two children: Mahati, their daughter, and Mohit, their son. Mohit is older than Mahati by two years and has a rare disease, and in spite of the best efforts of the Ghambirs, they could not make him better, but the couple never discussed their son in public. There was constant worry deep within; however, they were successful in hiding their concerns from the hospital staff and most of their relatives. None had the courage to ask, and after some time, their curiosity also reduced, leaving Mohit to his fate. Mahati, their daughter, is about 18 years old and looks 20+, tall, well-built, healthy-looking, and extremely beautiful. Her looks put the most modern heroines in Bollywood to shame. It was not just her beauty that attracted many; it was her nature and the way she interacted with others with so much warmth. Everyone in the hospital, especially young resident doctors, was attracted to her. There is a kind of grace that binds all, and she carried on naturally and with comfort. This surprised all, considering the nature of her mother, Dr. Swarna.

It was breakfast time in the morning, and Dr. Swarna felt everyone should necessarily join and discuss family matters. This is also due to the fact that both Gambhiers leave for the nursing home in the morning at 9.00 and were not sure when they would likely return, may be very late in the night, and many times Dr. Swarna slept at the hospital and returned in the morning. However, Swarna was always present for breakfast. In addition, the menu was carefully chosen to give the best both in terms of quality and quantity and was very meticulously planned. In fact, all in the house, including the servants, would be eagerly looking forward to Dr. Swarna leaving so that they could experience freedom and fresh air. In addition, table manners had to be exercised, and people had to be well dressed to have breakfast in the morning, though this is hated by all. While Dr. Swarna knows that no one likes her, she always thinks that she is doing good for the family.

No one knew what good was happening there, but for all the people who matter, it was an unnecessary discipline.

Mahati, more out of respect and fear, followed all these rules, and there was a strong undercurrent in her to disobey these rules. That day, a special BF was made, and Dr. Harpreet could not understand the exact reason but was waiting for something drastic to happen. It was a kind of silence, just before a cyclone.

On Friday, as a rare treat, Panditji, the chief cook, has made aloo paratha and pineapple halva, both favourites of Mahati. As usual, Mahati arrived at the dining table, fully dressed but late, and all were waiting for her to arrive, including Mohit. She was typically dressed in Punjabi style and had her college bag ready to go to the college.

The breakfast was served, and all were eating in silence, as if some unpleasant thing were likely to happen, and in anticipation, looking at their mobiles and not looking at each other. The following conversation followed.

"Mahati, how is your preparation for regular classes and coaching classes going on, and especially for NEET exams." asked Dr. Swarna, her mother.

"It's fine and normal, as expected;" was a crisp and short answer by Mahati.

"I understand that you are not attending the biological sciences classes and just showing interest in math and physics. Any specific reason?" shouted Dr. Swarna.

At this stage, it is important to note that few states allow students, like Maharastra students, to take PCMB so that they can appear for NEET or engineering courses, depending on their interest, though this is not allowed in some states.

Mahati joined IITJEE coaching classes without informing her parents, and this entire coaching was funded by her uncle, the brother of

Harpreet, without the knowledge of their parents. Mahati had decided to join the leading IITJEE coaching classes, where the class XII standard is also taken care of and they can focus more on IITJEE instead of spending too much time studying the state syllabus.

“I had discussed this with you well in the beginning and also explained the need for concentrating on NEET exams, and this will help you get admission to any good medical college. This will help you to do an MBA in hospital management at leading schools in the US. Subsequently, you can take care of the hospital administration.” said Swarna.

It appears that Swarna has worked on the entire career profile and placed all future dots, and Mahati has to connect the dots.

“I have mentioned then and now also that I am not interested in biological sciences, and I want to do aeronautical engineering from IIT Bombay.” said Mahati.

“Mahati, please do as I say, and this is good for your career and for our family,” said Swarna.

“Now listen to me; I have paid for all special coaching classes for PCB and also paid for coaching classes at home. This will help you prepare well for these highly competitive exams. My child, please listen to me; we are your parents, and we know what is good for you.” pleaded Dr. Swarna.

Parents always think that they are doing the best for their children, and no parent is an enemy of their own children. But what parents refuse to understand is the need to give freedom to their children at least after 18 years of age and guide them only if necessary. This conflict of interest is the main reason for the growing distance between parents and children. There are no easy solutions, and parents have to give their children freedom and allow them to learn from their mistakes.

Mahati says, “I had indicated to you earlier that I am not keen on continuing PCB, just because you have paid the fees. Don’t treat me like a scapegoat and impose your interest on me to become a doctor and manage the nursing home. I know this profession is noble, and you are doing the best service, but all at a cost. I am not like you. No matter what you say, I want to become an engineer, definitely not medicine, and I will not study for the NEET. At best, I can write the exam just to please you. I see both of you working from 9:00 a.m. to a bit late in the evening, sometimes even beyond midnight. I am not like you; please permit me to lead my life the way I want to lead; please ask for the refund of money you have paid, if that amount matters to you."

There was the sound of glass breaking from a very furious Swarna. She was sure that some of Mahati's friends had spoiled her and had been influenced by friends' advice.

Swarna threatened her daughter, Mahati, that she would cancel her admission to coaching classes for IITJEE and force her to join the NEET classes.

"Please also understand that admission to medicine is manageable by payment, and admission to IITs is not by payment. The competition is intense, and getting admission is next to impossible the way your studies are progressing." said Swarna.

At this stage, there was silence.

Mahati got up without having breakfast and left the house. She also said she did not want to use the car but only use public transport.

The entire atmosphere was very tense; now it was the turn of D. Harpreet to interfere and soothe Dr. Swarna, as patients must be waiting.

"Cancel all my appointments; Dr. Sheethal can handle them, and I want to rest myself, "said Swarna.

So she took the car and drove off to an unknown destination. This has not happened during the last 15 years, and all the staff and Dr. Harpreet were scared.

Harpreet followed Dr. Swarna along with a driver, and he knew that Swarna would be moving towards their outhouse, which was recently purchased and renovated at Alibhagh.

Dr. Harpreet comes from a middle-class background, and in fact, Dr. Swarna's father has helped him financially to complete all his studies. As he was living as per the wishes of Swarna's father, Swarna was married to Dr. Harpreet. He always felt obliged to reshape the family and help Swarna overcome the present crisis.

After a couple of hours, Dr. Harpreet says, "Please listen; Mahati is like you; maybe someone has influenced her; let her continue preparing for IITJEE and also write the NEET exam, as Mahati herself has agreed. If she gets admission to IITB, let her join, and in all probability she will not pass that exam and forget getting admission to IITB, Aeronautical Engineering. If she by chance gets admission, I have also checked many universities that offer an MBA in Hospital Management in the US, and at that time, Mahati might have matured, and she can be compelled to join an MBA in Hospital Management. If not, she will be assured of a medical seat in one of the leading medical colleges down south, and I have made all the arrangements. Please believe me, this is a win-win situation for all, and forcing Mahati may be counterproductive".

Many times, parents may pretend to listen to their children instead of voicing strong protests. Arguments will have strong reactions, and this might adversely affect the relationships. More than Dr. Swarna, Dr. Harpreet's love for his daughter was more intense, and he could not see tears in the eyes of Mahati. He also felt they badly needed an MBA in hospital management from the family side to run a big hospital, and in fact, an engineering degree would be an added qualification. As a last resort, Mahati could join a B.Tech. in bioengineering and related fields either in India or the USA and then do an MBA in hospital administration. In fact, the decision taken by her will motivate her to give her best, let her do what is most suitable for her, and evolve the future the way she wants.

This brought a temporary truce and peace to the house.

The elaborate answer from Dr. Harpreet convinced Dr. Swarna, and she knew that Dr. Harpreet was definitely a brilliant doctor, a good human being, and above all, very accommodating.

The only request from Dr. Swarna was to make Mahati do her MBA in hospital management in the USA, take care of their nursing home, and lead a happy life as per their wish.

At this stage, no one knows what the future is or how it will evolve.

Though the discussion ended at that stage, the thought process did not end for the Harpreet. He was very heavy on his heart and felt very lonely in spite of all his riches and very satisfying profession.

Harpreet got married to Swarna against the wishes of Harpreet's parents. Since Swarn's father was responsible for all his education, and after fully knowing the nature of Swarna, he got her married, thinking she would change after the marriage. This had distanced his parents, and not even once had Swarna visited his village, nor did his parents visit Mumbai. There were occasional phone calls, and he was sending some money to his parents without the knowledge of Swarna. His parents had no grudge against Swarna's family but had wished that she would fulfil some of the obligations of a daughter-in-law. In addition, his son had developed a severe form of autism for which no cure existed. Although this had devastated both families, life should have gone on, and when Mahati was born, for the first time, Harpreet's parents visited the Swana family, but enough respect was not given. This angered Harpreet. Wrong decisions, once taken, cause trouble till the last breath, and one has to live with it. Now, Harpreet thought and felt like going back to his village, and he left the car and mobile and just took the train to Jalander, and from there, a bus to his village. This has affected and mellowed down Mahati more than Swarna. As usual, you are stuck, and no amount of pressure on Swarna would help. Finally, for the sake of the children, on the advice of his parents, Harpreet has to return to Mumbai and start resuming his activities. This long and uninformed visit to Punjab had led to tensions in the family.

It was July, the rainy season was in full swing, and it was pouring cats and dogs in Mumbai. After the work was complete at the nursing home, Harpreet felt like driving down on his own, so he just left the hospital, gave rest to the driver, and decided to drive himself, generally not for more than 45 minutes. As it was pouring heavily and the road was not visible, he decided to stop the car for some time and wanted to get down from it and experience the rain himself. He took his umbrella and just moved to the footpath, where he started to see the flow of the water with its usual gurgling sound. He just noticed a small tea shop, and he had not taken tea on the footpath for years. He just ordered a cup of tea.

He could see about six people staying in that small hut covered with thick plastic. The couple, their parents, and their only daughter, and upon inquiry, the other boy was their brother's son, all from Bihar. The tea for the first time tasted good, and he just picked up a usual conversation. The couple works hard and earns about Rs 700 to Rs 1000 a day, and the children go to the nearby municipal school, and they have no grudges over anything. Their parents get treatment at the nearby municipal hospital, government rations, and all that they need to have a fulfilling life. There seems to be happiness, and they also send some money to the village and take care of their close relatives at their place. They seem to be content and happy with their lives. They have no concern about their tomorrow, and they know that too will pass by, so they are willing to face it with a sense of gratitude.

On the other hand, Dr. Harpreet had everything: a comfortable life, money, and respect in society. He was not happy and kept visiting doctors for his sleep deprivation problems. He just tried to analyse himself; he knew that he was a self-centred person. He married Swarna, not to show gratitude to Swarna's parents but to have control over the nursing home. He had forgotten his parents and was completely responsible for his problems. This was utter selfishness, and he was paying for all his misdeeds. In addition, he had engaged in many unethical practices to make money, and they were part of any medical practice, and this cumulative effect has destroyed his mental peace.

Now he knows that he is fully responsible for destroying his life and spoiling his mental peace, and he knows he cannot run away or stay; he has no option but to face all the mistakes he has made in his life. He married Swarna against the wishes of his parents, just to realise his dreams.

Harpreet was fully aware that Mahati was an above-average girl and would find it difficult to get admission to IITB, but she could get a rank in NEET and get admission to any private medical college. The problem is that Harpreet was fully aware; like her mother, Mahati is also adamant and will not listen. The most difficult part was accepting that it would be difficult to get into IITB and that more effort and coaching may be needed to get there. However, accepting that you do have enough mental strength is very important to channel the resources. Harpreet always felt tense; if something went wrong with the Mahati's career, this brought him more pain. He was highly disturbed, and his close attachment to his daughter started disturbing his peace of mind. He knows that at this juncture, nothing good can be done. He always felt a bit jealous of his parents, thinking that they were more happy than he was, and of so many of his friends in his village. He regretted that marrying Swarna was the biggest mistake, but it was too late now.

Mahati made all efforts to prepare for IITJEE and NEET, but she could not qualify for IITJEE but could get some meaningful rank in NEET for possible admission to a leading college in the South, and the decision to join MBBS was forced on her.

Mahati resisted joining MBBS in the south, as she was devastated that she was not getting admission of her choice at IITB. She now knew that she could not resist, pretended to have accepted a payment seat, and moved to the south to stay in a hostel.

She just spoke to her uncle one night and asked him to get admission to a leading coaching class for IITJEE in Kota, as a few of her own friends had joined. She just cancelled her medical seat, took some advanced payments from the university, and left for Kota for her try at IITJEE, an ambition of her lifetime. Mahati was so adamant at the time, a bit scared about her mother, and never felt the need to inform her parents.

Mahati, after settling down well at Kota, called up her father, Harpreet, and informed him about her decision to leave medicine and try for IITJEE once more. She also said that she was comfortable, giving her best, coaching was better, and the competition was very intense.

She also requested that her father not inform her mother, as she would be furious and may take drastic steps and play an emotional card.

Now, after speaking to his daughter, Mahati, Harpreet, was anticipating this to happen and was constantly worried about the daughter being alone and also anxious about the outcome of Mahati's second attempt at IITJEE if she was not qualified again. The only concern to Harpreet was whether Mahati would accept this gracefully and be normal. Assuming that this may not happen, Harpreet started worrying again, and especially Swarna might feel isolated. The helpless nature of parents due to their adamant decisions may not only spoil their lives but also keep their children's lives in danger.

Allow children to make their own decisions and learn from their mistakes. But this will never be learned by parents. It was time for Harpreet to consult a doctor regarding his highly disturbed sleep and lack of concentration at the office.

The main problem is the attachment of Harpreet to his daughter, Mahati. Dr. Harpreet, in spite of being an established doctor, was not willing to accept the possible defeat of his daughter in her second attempt. He was anticipating a problem that would occur in the future and suffering now for its consequences. This is a grave blunder many parents commit, and there seems to be no simple solution unless parents mature and allow things to evolve by themselves.

Mahati's uncle had made all arrangements for Mahati's comfortable stay at Kota.

Man proposes, and God disposes.

On the way to Kota from Jaipur

The plane from Mumbai has just landed in Jaipur. The Patels, an established business family, were facing the most awkward situations in their lives at the airport. They always thought they deserved the best and nothing less, especially for their only son, Bhavin Patel. This is because Bhavin had been exceptionally brilliant since childhood and always stood first in class from the first standard. Given this, many parents in their neighbourhood in Worli, Mumbai, wanted their sons/ daughters to be like Bhavin.

As they came out, Vipin Patel, Bhavin's father, wanted his son to rest at the airport, and he moved out to fetch an air-conditioned sedan for their journey to Kota. All parents wanted to give their best to their children, and in the process, unintentionally made them dependent. Out of love, parents often do not test their children's capabilities and pamper them unnecessarily.

Finally, they identified a car, an Innova, a recent model after careful scrutiny of many cars. The driver had picked up the heavy luggage and tried his best to place it in the back; a few items were kept on top and tied with a rope to prevent them from falling during the long journey of over six hours. Bhavin's mother moved to the back seat of the car, as did Vipin. Bhavin always preferred the front seat and requested the driver to increase the air-conditioning, as it was very hot. There were constant demands to stop at regular intervals for food, and the driver had no option but to oblige. In fact, it took more than 8 hours to reach Kota. As they were moving, the sun was at its fiercest, and the AC was not sufficient for its occupants.

All were lost in their thoughts, especially Bhavin, who felt responsible for his failure and wanted to be more committed this time. He also felt he had let down his parents and was quite upset as they travelled to Kota. This time, he thought that he must make use of the best coaching in Kota during his stay and also try to make the best friends who are better than him and learn quickly. Now, Bhavin had realised that the only way to learn quickly was to interact with others.

Many believe that learning is a one-way process, but they never know that sharing knowledge with others is essential. In fact, during the sharing, you learn more, which helps you become better and more confident.

The Gujarati Family

The family consists of Vipin Patel, the head of the family, his wife Meera Patel, and their only son, Bhavin. They had several decades of experience in business in the diamond industry. They stayed in the very posh area of Worli, Mumbai, and also owned several flats in Powai. It was not exactly clear what their diamond business was to several outsiders; however, they were very respected, as many leading personalities and politicians visited their showroom in Kalabadevi, Mumbai. They understood the diamond business quite well and also developed the necessary infrastructure at several places in Gujarat and showrooms at different places in India. They had more than 500 employees on their payroll, and many worked on daily wages. There were several rumours that there were several income tax raids at their flat in Worli, but no action was taken, possibly due to their strong connection with politicians.

Vipin is a Maharashtrian, was by nature very ambitious, and had no talent. Meera met Vipin at one of the marriage functions, and Vipin was introduced to Meera. Vipin fell in love, as did Meera, and their marriage was a kind of arranged marriage that had the acceptance of both families. Meera's father had already established his business in Mumbai and, in fact, was looking for a trustworthy person to run his business at different places in Mumbai and at different places in India and abroad. He found Mr. Vipin, a decent, sincere, and also hard-working commerce graduate. Mr. Vipin was also willing to move into Patel's family and take care of the business. During the process, he changed his name to Vipin Patel instead of Meera, taking the traditional family name of Vipin. This was Vipin's way of showing his commitment to the Patels family and his love and affection for Meera.

Not many had studied up to graduation in the Patels family, and it was no necessity to study as their main objective was to procure raw diamonds from anywhere in the world, do precise polishing at their workshop in Surat, make jewels, and carry on with their business. Vipin had learned the tricks of this trade, travelled extensively abroad, and had become an expert in this business. In addition, they had other businesses in Surat and had enough funds to start new showrooms in different places in India. They had no interest in their only son, Bhavin, studying, earning money, and making a career. For them, studying was a waste of time, and instead, learning in trades or business would provide more money than the best educated person could earn. A regular job could never be satisfying. In fact, the quality of average business is very tough and revolves around profit and loss statements. What they wanted was to earn more at any cost, even by all unfair means. The Patels family had the necessary intelligence to invest judiciously and enhance their income.

The successful business of the Patels is not relevant to our story.

Now, let us move towards the education graph of Bhavin Patel.

In general, Bhavin was a gifted, intelligent, and hard-working student who also got an NTSE scholarship at X standard. Many parents in the circle believed that their children should be like Bhavin.

This family had the necessary funds to purchase a seat in any of the IITS if it was available for sale. The Patel family never realised that several things in life are obtained through hard work, reputation, and commitment, and these are not available for sale.

The Vipin family was quite happy about the success of their son, Bhavin. They wanted Bhavin should take up the commerce subjects in XII and then do B.Com. and CA. This would help the family business grow. The Patels always felt the need for a family man to handle finances, as professionals are demanding and not dependable. In addition, Patels never understood the tax structure and the intricacies, and they always suspected that they would be taken for a ride if handled by the experts. If Bhavin could complete his CA, it would help the company and grow their family business.

At this stage, it is important to share the extreme love between Bhavin and his mother, Meera. In general, there is a strong relationship between mothers and their sons, and this is something extraordinary. Right from KG to class IIX, all Meena did was take her son to school in her car and bring him back, even though there was a school bus. In addition, takes tiffin to the school on the pretext of seeing her son and giving him hot food. Feeding Bhavin was an obsession, and Meera liked this job and thought that she was the best mother. This excessive love towards her son made Bhavin depend heavily on his mother, and interactions with other friends, especially socialising skills, were very limited. This made Bhavin obese, and he had a few health issues right from childhood. No amount of advice from her own family doctor or family members would help. This has made Bhavin irritable, emotional, and very sensitive. With time, Bhavin has developed into an insecure person, and no one can predict his reaction to a particular situation. This had spread a kind of fear in the house, and his parents had started to adjust to his demands more to make him unduly happy. This was disastrous for any growing adult.

Time had different plans for them.

It was in one of the casual functions in the family, and Vipin's sister's son Rajesh commented that taking science subjects and passing IITJEE was tough, and not even a single member of their family had tried or written IITJEE. Rajesh unknowingly challenged Bhavin. This attracted Bhavin, and he said, "I will do it and take up science subjects and try IITJEE, but at present, I am not interested in taking forward the business at this stage."

In addition, Bhavin said, "I like challenges and show you all that I am capable."

This has taken a serious turn, and the decision appears to be irrevocable. Many times, without knowing the consequences, we make comments that could be detrimental and have consequences. In this case, the Patels family was affected, and for good or bad, only they could predict.

Bhavin opted for M, P, and C in his XII standard and joined reputed coaching classes in Mumbai against the wishes of his parents. They felt that their son had not taken a good decision, and this might affect their family business and also the professional career of Bhavin. Being in the business, the Patel family does not know the magnitude of the problems or how demanding the IITJEE would be. Ignorance is blessing, and the Patels family was indulgent and sure that he would come back to the family business later and learn the nuance of family business.

Bhavin was an intelligent boy and could understand the difficulty levels of IITJEE, so he started taking coaching classes very seriously. He felt mathematics was extremely difficult, and he was feeling the pain at several stages of preparation and was helpless. During the preparation, Bhavin tried his best to give his best and also take private coaching, as finances to hire private tuition were never an issue.

In spite of the best efforts by Bhavin, he could not clear IITJEE, and to keep his prestige intact, he decided to move to Kota, join the best coaching classes, and make one more attempt—in fact, the last attempt—to pass IITJEE and also get a good rank to join Computer Engineering at IITB. He was fully aware of the mistakes he had committed during the earlier preparation and decided to overcome these difficulties and also increase the intensity and seriousness with which he cleared IITJEE. This is the real strength of any student—to know his weaknesses and the methods to overcome them. This is an important step to success.

The Patils family made all arrangements for Bhavin to have a comfortable stay at Kota. The family did not feel comfortable initially but got used to the quality of life at Kota, only to keep their son, Bhavin, happy. The Patels family never understood the intricacies involved but kept themselves happy. At times, ignorance is really bliss, and the Patels family is not an exception.

Chapter II

The Struggle

It is natural for students to be attached to the end results, as the mind works only on profit and loss as it is trained that way.

The mind must be constantly trained to enjoy the journey, the process of studying, and a dispassionate attitude towards the end results. This training is much harder than passing IITJEE. This training will eventually lead to better concentration during preparation and enhanced delivery during the examination.

Imagine a driver driving in difficult terrain during the night on a rainy day. The driver's attention should be on the journey and not worrying about reaching the destination.

The mind is always in a state of action, and we do not use our mind; the mind uses us. An impure Mind can be your enemy, and a Pure mind is your friend.

Testing Times

Student life is the best part of life and, without any exception, should be made enjoyable. But it is not always true, and for selected students, life is very stressful when their ambitions and expectations do not match their talents.

It is always felt that the present is prosaic, looks very daunting, and expects all to perform their best by maintaining a very high degree of discipline that is too consistent, which is not possible, however great the ambition and commitment are.

A few troubling aspects are recognising and analysing the problem and the peer pressure, which many find hard to cope with. In addition, many students may need more hours of sleep, control excessive hunger, and, above all, reduce their usage of social media, which is a major aberration for any time management. The thought and fear of failure are always dangling over them, which may make many students very uncomfortable. Finally, as adolescence kicks in, resulting in uncontrolled romantic thoughts and the urge to mix with other gender partners, the uncontrolled lusty thoughts do not wane but become stronger as they face the critical moment.

The constant control of parents, who at times are too demanding, makes life stressful. Many feel trapped between parental love and the demands of themselves, which propels these individuals into zones of extreme discomfort.

The three families, Vishnues, Gambhirs and Patels arrived at Kota.

Madhav, Bhavin and Mahati stayed at Kota and started looking for success on their second IITJEE attempt.

Life at Kota

Kota, like any typical Indian city, is not the best place to live. It is bubbling with students, and this may be the main reason for its economic growth. The temperature is extreme, and in the summer it is very high and intolerable, while in the winter it is quite low. The nearby thermal power plant makes it very dusty, and the presence of a nuclear power plant makes it on the international map, hence the city has its own special importance. No one really knows why this city has become a hub for coaching centres for many competitive exams in India. It is not that many students pass from this city because many students study from this city. It was felt that initially there was a person who had a decent ability to solve any problems given in the IITJEE exams, and he had enough confidence and passion to teach so that his students would make it to IITs. This passion later turned into money-making machines, and the mushrooming of training institutes has grown to teach yet another method for making money. Now, this is not limited to Kota alone, and there are many such coaching centres in major cities all around India.

In India, there are very few people who make money, and not many are from the service or working sector. Its very selected few, by unscrupulous means, make money, and there are no easy ways to distinguish between scrupulous and unethical ways. The selected are those who are involved in building religious resorts, education institutes (coaching institutes), medical professionals, the cinema industry, and finally, the business industry. It is by no means to say all the above categories are unethical, but many fall into this category and become rich. It is needless to say most coaching institutes thrive on the fees paid by the failed students. All this is related to attracting more students by showing the number of students passed in all leading newspapers. Not many institutes show the number of students admitted and the number of students passed, and this ratio is ridiculously small. This is not to undermine the importance of coaching in shaping a student's career or improving their learning skills.

In addition, the award of merit scholarships or awards to those students who have cleared IITJEE or got top ranks is another headline in the leading newspapers, and this attracts both the students and parents. Finally, the pay package that some students (to be honest, very few) receive after completing any of the IITs is again a topic of discussion and tempts many undecided students and parents to jump on this bandwagon of competition. In India, parents are willing to go to any extent to provide the best education possible, on the pretext of self-gratification that they have done their best for their children. Several parents sell their properties, gold ornaments, and cooking vessels to finance their children's education. This is after fully knowing the pass percentage is so low. Many coaching institutes use this as an emotional card and admit students after fully knowing that their chances of passing are too low. Many students and parents do not understand that their responsibility is not just the willingness to pay but also checking the suitability of the students to withstand the extreme stress they have been subjected to during coaching.

There is a communication gap between the students and parents as they move along the course preparation related to success, and many times the children keep silent and give false hope to their parents that there is a chance for them to crack the exams. On the other hand, parents are also aware that their children may not pass. There is a mental conflict in parents' minds, and finally, parents convince themselves that there is a possibility of passing, and if somehow their child clears, the next path is going quite smoothly. This communication gap between parents and children is not new. This may be the success or failure stories of many.

What is most disturbing is that if the stress during coaching reaches a high point, it may adversely affect students and may result in several mental health complications. This is not part of a success story. Not many coaching institutes, leading newspapers, parents, and even students highlight this, and this is really the most painful story.

Let me relate a well-known story. There was a big banyan tree, and a scorpion was living in the small hole in its trunk. Everyone, out of curiosity, used to insert his finger and pretend as if nothing had happened, even though he was experiencing extreme pain. This pretence was to expect his other friend to also experience this pain. Similarly, none of the failed or derailed students or parents expressed their anguish in public.

Let us not spend more time at the coaching institutes, and this is a matter for more discussion in the next chapter.

The hostel accommodation and single-room accommodation close to the coaching institute are of immense attraction to both the students and parents. Not many coaching classes have hostels, and this investment is too huge, and not many enter these areas. Instead, they have their own huge buildings with modern teaching facilities and even different types of architecture to attract students. To be honest, most of the institutes may not have their own buildings, as they are not sure if they can sustain the competition from other established coaching institutes.

Now, the land owners, who are willing to rent out their accommodation to the students coming from different parts of India, are so mean that they have made dangerous illegal construction and used each and every inch of available space in very narrow rooms with very meagre facilities. They charge extraordinary deposits and rent and put the best rented accommodations in Mumbai to shame. Some of the landlords had made enough money and made more money than the best students passed out from the IITs. Thanks to the mushrooming of coaching institutes at Kota, everyone—the landlords, coaching institutes, advertising agents, and local shop vendors—makes money at the expense of the parents. This is sometimes so disgusting, yet many are helpless. The less said, the better it is.

Now coming to our story, a ground-plus-two stories building close to the leading coaching institute is more relevant to us. The owner, Mr. Ajay Bansal, and his family—his wife, two sons, and a daughter—live on the ground floor. The first floor has six very small rooms without restroom facilities. The second floor has washrooms, one small room adjacent to the washrooms, and two fairly large rooms with an attached kitchen and a bathroom with a balcony facing the market street. Bansal has made separate entry to these two big rooms, which are generally given to girl students. The boys staying on the first floor use the second-floor bathroom facility, which has a separate entrance from the back. The small room, which is actually a dump store room, Bansal has vacated and renovated as a study room adjacent to the bathrooms, both out of greed to get more rent and also under the pretext of helping students. The water is limited and is available for a limited period. He will charge for electricity and any other amenities that were fixed in the room, which may have an air conditioner. It becomes impossible to study on the second floor. Bansal has fixed split ACs and given them to those who are willing to pay exorbitant rent and also to girl students. Bansal has kept a servant to look after the needs of the students and a small water filter so that students do not fall sick due to contaminated water. The ground floor has the water filter. However, both rooms on the second floor have an aquaguard water filter fixed along the corridor and are not accessible to other students on the first floor. The second-floor students can get access to the aqua guard water, a luxury when the outside temperature is touching 48 °C. No wonder only serious students who are willing to pay the rent, fees to the coaching institutes, and hotel bills make an attempt to stay at these places.

Mahati's uncle knew a person in Kota and, through his contacts, got admission to possibly the best coaching centre as per her performance in the entrance test conducted by this coaching institute at several places in India. Now, most of these coaching centres, depending on the capacity of their buildings, may admit students many times above 5,000 in a given year. This number includes two years of in-house coaching, one year of intense coaching for fresh students, and one year of intense coaching for students writing for the second time. This is relevant for our story as many students writing for the second time are more successful as they have tasted defeat and have a passion to qualify. In order to limit this number, they conduct entrance tests at selected places to choose the best among those available at any given time. The prestigious coaching centres do not generally give direct admission to any student as they do not have any infrastructure to handle, though they may be interested. In fact, the coaching classes run from 6 a.m. to 11 p.m.

Based on the chosen coaching institute by Mahati, her uncle had booked the second-floor room, which had some facilities. He had also arranged for a cook for her so that she could continue to eat home-cooked food. The rent for this room was never an issue for Mahati's uncle, as the safety, proximity of coaching, and above all, providing the necessary comfort to Mahati were more important. Though Mahati was not very happy with that room and looking at the other rooms, which had practically no other facilities, she agreed to stay in that room for the next year. Generally, one has absolute and relative comparisons with peers, and if you have underperformed to your capacity but made better than your competitor, it brings in some selfish thoughts.

The second room, with all the facilities, had been booked for Bhavin, and the Patel family decided to station their mother, Meera, there so that she could continue to shower abundant love on her son and also take care of cooking. This was a lifelong ambition of Meera to stay with her son, and by the grace of the Lord, it was fulfilled. Though Bhavin was not happy about his mother's continuous stay with him, he had to accept it, as eating out was never an option. Initially, the landowner, Bansal, was not willing to rent to a boy, and as his mother was staying with his son and was willing to pay more rent, Bansal finally agreed to rent another spacious room to the Patels family. In fact, Bhavin also joined the same coaching centre as Mahati, and there was some sort of understanding between both families.

Now Madhav was in two minds to shift to the small room on the second floor; in fact, he would have preferred a lower-rent room away from the coaching centre, but due to the summer, travelling was an issue even with a bicycle. His room was very modest, with a table, chair, study lamp, a book stand, and a cot. The only problem is the constant noise during the usage of washrooms by the boys from the first floor, and Madhav had no option but to adjust, taking in a short stay of 10 months and also relatively lower rent. Vishnu and Madhav could hardly sleep in that room due to the very limited carpet space. Vishnu had made arrangements for eating in a nearby Aggarwal mess with an advance payment. Vishnu tried his best to initiate some conversation with the Patels family and Mahati's uncle, but was not successful. The reasons for this will be known as we move along.

Life was very tough at Kota due to the summer, and the quality of food served at restaurants, hotels, and private eateries was too spicy and generally not healthy. In addition, the facilities at this Bansals apartment were of the barest minimum, and most students felt like running away to their native places, but for their strong ambition to get admission at IITs.

There were about six boys on the first floor, mostly from different states in India, and their story is not relevant to us. However, they kept using the washroom facilities available on the second floor, disturbing Madhav's concentration, and at times, loud noise was also a big nuisance for Madhav. However, beggars cannot be choosers but have to get used to a bit of this, as the very purpose of staying was to attend the classes, keep studying, and get confidence to write IITJEE.

Coaching Institutes

Most coaching institutes are not there for charity, and they have their own agendas. Their survival depends on the selection of the best students available anywhere in India and training them to pass the IITJEE. This would ensure the admission of their minimum number of students in the coming years.

Many leading coaching institutes conduct written exams all over India based on the XII standard, especially for those students who could not clear the IITJEE for the first time, and they have their own criteria to identify and give admission. If the institute feels a particular student is likely to clear IITJEE, they go out of the way to offer a fellowship and several other facilities to get admitted in their institutes. This is just like poaching, and most of the institute administrators clearly knew that students were likely to bring laurels to their institute. This is because the faculty is generally shared by most of the coaching classes, and through the faculty, the performance of selected students at an institute is estimated even before writing the IITJEE.

Generally, students selected based on the all-India entrance exams are divided into different sections and subsections and grouped so that nearly all performances are brought together. For example, all students who have gotten more than 80% of their marks in the entrance exams are grouped as the X1 batch. Getting more than 80% of marks in these exams is not an easy task as the difficulty level is kept quite high, and those students who have worked hard for two years and could not clear IITJEE for several unknown and known reasons. However, their admission may require a minimum effort from the institutes to clear the IITJEE. Accordingly, from X1 to X10, Y1 to Y10, and Z1 to Z10 batches are made. It is needless to say that students admitted to the Z1 to Z10 batches are not likely to pass but pay the fees, and the coaching institutes survive on batches from X5 to X10, Y1 to Y10, and Z1 to Z10 batches. Everyone in the administration of these institutes might know that these students may not pass, but the institutes run on the funds collected from the failed students. Even assuming about 100 students in each section, there are close to 3000 students who are repeaters and working hard to make their chance to get admitted to IITS. It is no surprise; there might be many alphabets (apart from X, Y, and Z, there may be P, Q, and R, and no one really knows how many students joined a repeater batch).

The admission to fresh batches, who have completed VIII, IX, X, and XI, and are admitted based on another exam, is a different story and will not be relevant to the present story. In fact, there are many coaching institutes that coach students for entrance exams to gain admission to the best coaching centres. This is another process and holds no significance for us.

After the students get admission to these batches, X1 to Z10, there is an internal exam nearly identical in pattern to IITJEE. Based on the marks obtained, ranks are allocated, and a major reshuffle is made in batch allocation. This seems to be a logical and rational way to provide a fair chance for students to move from the Y and Z batches to the X batch. It also allows for a reshuffling of students in the X1 to X10 batches. It's also possible for a student from the X5 batch to move to the X2 batch, and a student from the X1 batch could move to the X3 batch. This is the beginning, which can be quite challenging for most students. The fittest and the best survive, and most of these institutes treat students as guinea pigs. There is no time, and coaching institutes have no other option as they have to provide the best teaching faculty, who are likely to clear IITJEE. There is constant comparison at the initial stages to weed out underperforming students. This discrimination reduces the chance for even X1 batch students to interact with X2 students. The competition is so severe that even X1 students will hardly interact with students from their own batch. This fosters an untouchable attitude in the minds of many students, which remains in the system and will continue throughout their further studies. This intense competition among students unknowingly fosters selfish interests, discouraging the sharing of information. This underlying current, competition of this magnitude, undermines the enthusiasm for learning.

The reasons students prefer to move to upper batches and settle in X1 or X2 batches are that classes are held at convenient hours, the best faculty with a minimum of ten or more years of experience are selected for teaching, and extreme care is taken in evaluating these students and providing additional teaching and assignments if necessary. Administrators are fully aware that students only pass from X1 to X4 batches, and the success story of their institute and future admissions depend solely on these students.

It is important to narrate an experiment that was conducted and how the behaviour of students changes as you keep discriminating. Based on nearly the same IQ level among students of 100, a group of ten students was picked arbitrarily, and they were given a false impression, indicating that the selection criteria were based on merit. The students who had nearly the same IQ were made to believe by the system that they were better than the rest of the ninety students. In fact, after some time, though nearly identical coaching was given to all 100 students, these students belonging to ten batches performed better. Hence, discriminating against each other may have a far-reaching effect on the psychology of students. The administrators of these coaching institutes understand this but plead helplessness. Discrimination is the only weapon to initiate an unhealthy competition to excel.

Needless to say, any students from any of the batches (X, Y, and Z) can clear IITJEE, but for this discrimination in the teaching and care many students find it hard to move to higher batches from Z to Y to X, as the further exams conducted later will not help in the major reshuffle. Many students know this and feel helpless. Most students are less than 20 years old, and staying alone (no parental care) is not mature enough to handle the discrimination of the coaching institutes and the stress due to the reshuffling of the batches in the beginning. Several students face serious stress-related problems. They can neither express this to their colleagues nor to their parents, as this further increases the stress of the parents, which most students do not want. This discrimination among students at a tender age will have far-reaching consequences for further studies in the future. Due to limited seats, coaching institutes may not always be blamed, as they have to survive on their passing percentage of students.

Parents feel they have done their best, but the responsibilities of parents should not end there. They should see if there are any behavioural changes after admission of their children, and if so, they should consider taking them away from these highly competitive and ambitious environments and getting them admitted to a normal school. In fact, this helps the students, and parents should not consider this a defeat but applaud themselves for the courage they have shown and also express this to other parents. The coaching institutes have no mechanism to take care of individual students (except X batch students) nor a willingness to address the students emotional issues. Now, before embarking on such a high-octane journey as climbing Everest for the first time, parents should make an assessment of their children to see if this journey is worth it, as they may lose their children forever. Severe competition is not good for many students, and many may not have the necessary mechanisms to handle stress, get derailed, and become a burden for themselves as they move along in further studies. It might take years of medical attention for a few students to become normal, and extreme caution must be exercised before embarking on this competitive exam and coaching at Kota for admission to any of the leading colleges, either engineering at NITS, IITS, government colleges, or AIIMS.

The real soul of any teaching institute is not the buildings or teaching aids, but mostly the faculty, and this is a very rare commodity. Many faculties are past students who have passed IITJEE at about 10 years of age with a certain rank and are now willing to return to Kota and start teaching. Many institutes advertise for faculty recruitment in leading newspapers with fairly attractive enumerations and other benefits and recruit them for teaching. The biggest problem faced by the institutes is retaining the best faculty, as they are constantly poached by other institutes. The demand goes up, and so does the pay package, and sometimes the remuneration and perks that are provided are so large that they might bring shame to many CEOs in the leading corporate world. The problem is that the faculty also tastes the power of the money and success stories made by the institutes, and they plan their own private institutes and poach the best students from the X1 batch with attractive fellowships. There is a constant struggle between the coaching institutes, the faculty, and the students, and this might bring in some kind of semi-equilibrium, and this whole process might work against the well-being and performance of the students.

Imagine how the system works and makes many helpless, but the utmost caution should be exercised by parents and students. Students need handholding until they join any professional courses and help them in their difficult times, but with the utmost empathy. Later on, allow them to handle their problems and face all the consequences of their right or wrong decision. There has to be a limit for parents to love their children; this helps their children take the right decision with immense thought. This will help them to take any stress that will be there as they move along their lives, and this will continue to grow as they are responsible for their destinies.

There are close to 23 IITs, and they may at best admit around 25000 to 30000 students at IITs and not more. The students who write the IITJEE are in the range of 8,00,000 to 10,00,000, and this means only 2 to 3% is the success rate of passing, which is even smaller compared to the top ten universities in the USA. This also means that not getting selected in the IITJEE could be due to the performance of the day and might not reflect on the overall competition and capability of a student. This must be understood, and this helps to cope with the situation when the results are not favorable.

Imagine an exam has to be conducted to select only 2–3% of students based on their performance based on the earlier single-written exams or a small variation in recent times based on two-stage exams. In all these exams, a basic understanding of the concepts, speed, accuracy, and depth of understanding are necessary tools to discriminate among the students. As we move along, there are several students who did not write IITJEE but are doing well as they are. Hence, the exams are set on some pattern, and the coaching institutes start working on these models and adjust the mode of coaching and preparation to suit a student who wants to pass the exams but does not necessarily understand the concept. This must be clear in the minds of parents and students. Clearing IITJEE is definitely no mean achievement, but not getting through means nothing. Leave this and take up engineering or any other professional course of his choice, and the student's success in the future depends more on his performance than on his failure at IITJEE. Forget the past and move on is the life motto; this must be emphasised to the students by their parents, and not passing means nothing except that you have made an attempt sincerely, and many successes are there in the future. Life is beautiful, and just enjoy every moment. This must be the lesson for all students.

Now let us return to our story and try to understand where the problem is.

Bhavin and Mahati are the best students, and they felt highly depressed about not passing their exams. Both were best at their school and never stood second in their classes and always performed best, and this has developed an intellectual arrogance in their minds, and this recent happening of not clearing an exam has developed a feeling of self-doubt and a sense of helplessness after not clearing the IITJEE.

On the other hand, Madhav had many reasons for not qualifying in the IITJEE, and that may be the reason for his admission to the X5 batch and not to the X1 to X4 batches. Though he had a good understanding of physics and mathematics, chemistry was not interesting to him. In spite of his best efforts, he could not spend enough time reading chemistry. Sometimes we are our own enemies, and this is one such rare example.

Based on their performance at the coaching institutes, Bhavin was in the X1 batch, Mahati was in the X2 batch, and Madhav was in the X5 batch. This distribution or allocation of batches may be meaningful for the coaching institutes, but it appears to not be genuinely testing the students capabilities. Immediately after the internal exams, a major reshuffling was carried out by the coaching institutes. Bhavin was sent to the X2 batch and Mahati was maintained in the X2 batch, but Madhav moved to the X3 batch. This means Madhav had performed better than several hundred students and in fact secured more marks than Bhavin and Mahati, but the reshuffling was based on the aggregate of marks between the entrance and the internal exams. This never disturbed Madhav, but Bhavin was highly furious, as he felt that Madhav moved from the X5 batch to the X3 batch and has secured more marks than many X1 batch students. In fact, Madhav could have just moved to the X1 batch, taking purely the internal exam, which was much tougher than the entrance exam. Now, nothing counts, and students have to maintain and keep working hard and try to retain their batches to get better coaching.

The performance of Madhav was noticed by the physics teacher, who suggested to the administration that Madhav be promoted to the X1 batch, but the system did not agree. However, Madhav was called to the office and warned that he should start working hard in chemistry so that he could pass IITJEE, as this exam consisted of a minimum pass in all three subjects, and after passing all the exams, only the ranks were made. In spite of several warnings, Madhav could not spend sufficient time studying chemistry; few are strong, and they can't change because they are naturally like that. Few are great; few are great by action, and for a few, greatness is trusted. Madhav belonged to a special class; he knew his limitations but was not willing to work on his weaknesses.

What worried most of the students at the coaching classes was the fear of failure, and this was more so for the students who were writing the exams for the second time. In addition, the parents and their relatives, who mattered, were also concerned about the success, and the parents could never express it explicitly to their children, and the children could hardly say or discuss it with their parents. This is sometimes life fighting in darkness for many students. This fear of failure, and especially their peers who have already joined IITB and are in touch with the students who are at Kota, Sometimes success brings a sense of confidence, and sometimes failure brings a sense of fear, and even the best students in the X1 batch face this. This additional pressure, to some extent, may have a positive effect, but if it exceeds the limits, it can be detrimental. All students have to cope with this pressure; unfortunately, it becomes unbearable as the exams get closer.

Attraction between Bhavin and Mahati

Bhavin and Mahati were in the X2 batch, and their class timings were the same. They were going to the coaching classes together. In addition, Mahati was good at chemistry and Bhavin was excellent at both physics and mathematics, and they were sharing notes, spending time to clear their doubts, and also doing combined studies.

Mahati was staying alone with the cook from Mumbai and had all the freedom to choose her life the way she felt. However, Bhavin's mother and a cook were always there to take care of Bhavin's minute-to-minute requirements. Even a calling bell was removed intentionally, as this would be a disturbance while studying. This was a kind of protective environment; Bhavin at times disliked it but was accepting as this care helped him to spend more time with his preparation. Bhavin was going out of his way to help Mahati with her studies, and this was not liked by Mahati, who wanted to learn all her self as this was the only way to think independently and solve real-time problems during the examinations.

Like any modern girl, Mahati was brought up in a fairly high-ranking society, was not orthodox, was always willing to speak on any topic, and was generally very friendly to all, including Bhavin. There was no special attachment or aversion towards any.

Bhavin's grandma, who stayed in Ahmedabad, had a hip fracture. Meera was the only daughter and was attached to her mother. Meera decided to rush to Ahmadabad to be by the side of her mother, and this was a major operation that required a prolonged stay for Meera in Ahmadabad. This helped Bhavin find some free time, and he wanted to do several things, which he could not do due to his mother's presence.

Bhavin and some of his friends decided to go to a nearby resort about 6 km from their place, and they decided to hire a vehicle. Bhavin decided to host a party on Sunday after the test exam conducted by the coaching institute. Many of his friends, mostly from his batch X2 and a few from X1, were also invited, and they wanted to taste the smell and possibly drink alcohol as they were all over 18 years old. They may have to carry their date of birth certificate as proof. In addition, there was also a possibility that Bhavin may be promoted to the X1 batch, and this was a celebration mode. He had pride and, above all, a sense of insecurity about anyone who performed better than him in any area. He was working very hard to overcome his deficiencies and tried his best to excel. The only problem he had at times was that he lacked the originality to solve a problem, especially in physics, and this drawback was known to him but never accepted. Once, there was a problem given in the area of the moment of inertia as a challenge to only X1 batch students, and not many could even attempt to forget about solving it. In order to test her intelligence and originality, he marked that copy to Mahati with a request to solve. She found it hard, and she in turn sent it to Madhav to solve, and within 30 minutes, the answer was there, and Madhav was quick to solve with the intention of taking a challenge. Mahati could not understand the answer, so she learned the method over the phone and sent the answers to Bhavin. She also said that Madhav solved that problem rather quickly. This was the beginning and end of the relationship between Madhav and Bhavin, and Bhavin never liked him as he was from the X3 batch. The problem is that even after getting the solution, Bhavin could not understand the method adopted. This disturbed him, and he started disliking, or rather hating, Madhav. Finally, Mahati took Madhav to Bhavin's room and asked him to explain to both of them. Since Mahati had brought Madhav, Bhavin kept quiet, and Madhav explained with the utmost seriousness with the intention to help and not to show his attitude. Now, Bhavin knew well that Madhav was extraordinary and was good at physics, and students from the X3 batch were not bad and could give tough competition. Bhavin thought of exploiting Madhav's talent more often without giving anything in return. Madhav could understand Bhavin's real intentions from his questions and attitude, but he decided to be friendly and help in these areas where he was good. In the area of geometry or calculus, Bhavin was quite good, never showed interest, and always mentioned that he was not clear with concepts. This difference in their approach to cooperating never missed the attention of Mahati.

Bhavin invited Mahati to the party on Sunday, and she could join as a few more girls were also coming. She would feel comfortable, and the travel had been arranged. Bhavin also indicated that the party was only for students from the X1 and X2 batches. Mahati understood that he did not want to call Madhav as he was from the X3 batch. Mahati agreed, and they had fun that night. However, one thing that disturbed Mahati was a bit of misbehaviour by Bhavin, for which Bhavan apologised. Matters settled down quickly, and both behaved as if no one was hurt and continued their relationship as usual as if nothing had happened.

Mahati was quite clear that she was dependent on Bhavin for physics and mathematics, and any kind of gesture from her side may disturb the friendship, which may be to her great disadvantage. All are selfish at heart, and they know exactly what they want from the system. That may be the reason; it is next to impossible to judge the thought process in the minds of females, and Mahati was not an exception. After that small incident, Bhavin started developing feelings towards Mahati, and any advancements were not allowed by Mahati, and this was assumed to be normal by Bhavin. He continued to impress Mahati and tried his best to be friendly, and Mahati always pretended that she was impressed, and she was sure that she never liked Bhavin or approved of his behaviour.

Mahati was always in two minds about the choice between Bhavin and Madhav. Bhavin was slightly on the heavier side due to his uncontrolled eating habits, was shrewd and cunning, and was too selfish. He wanted to win at any cost. It was clear that Bhavin was sufficiently rich and was sure to do well, and at times he pretended to be very accommodating. In addition, there is some familiarity between the Mahati's uncle and the parents of Bhavin. Girls mature very fast and will express their choice at an appropriate time. It was not clear what was going on in the mind of Mahati; however, Bhavin had already made several advances that were not equally reciprocated by Mahati, and this was very disappointing to Bhavin. He continued to impress Mahati by helping her more and spending more time on the pretext of combined studies. But somewhere deep in his mind, Bhavin had the feeling that Mahati was at times quite friendly to Madhav, and this was a cause of serious concern to Bhavin. Bhavin's main intention in coming to Kota against all odds was to work hard and get into the IITs of his choice. In addition, if you could impress Mahati, it was an added benefit. Any love with selfish motives may at times look possible, but a long-term relationship looks difficult.

Natural liking between Madhav and Mahati

It was one of the worst afternoons in Kota, and the temperature was close to 46 °C.

Madhav and Mahati decided to go to the nearby institute by bus to learn about the book, which contained selected problems in physics, chemistry, and mathematics and hints to solve these numerical problems. The institute had recently launched, and the institute has made it available to all by payment. This was possibly a strategy to advertise their institute. This was the first time Mahati had entered a bus in Kota, and she wanted to have some entertainment and also have company with Madhav. The bus was fairly full.

All the passengers seem to be disturbed due to the summer heat and the slow movement of the bus due to the very heavy traffic. There were heated arguments between passengers, and it appeared all the problems in the world were loaded onto that bus. A few students were upset about their performance; a young couple was upset with their child as the child was crying very loudly; another old woman was annoyed for reasons best known to her; another family was taking their daughter to the hospital with a very high fever; and finally, a pregnant woman was suffocating as there were no seats to sit in nor had anyone offered a seat to her. Just then, a lady in her 40s entered the bus with a basket full of flowers, including roses, chavanti, jasmine, and other varieties. The fragrance filled the bus, and this changed the atmosphere of the bus. All seemed to relax. The bus conductor, after giving tickets to all, out of the blue, requested that the lady to give flowers. Without a murmur, she shared a rose in a small basket that this woman always carried.

The bus conductor approached all the passengers in the bus and gave them a rose and asked them to pray in their minds and mentally offload that problem in that flower. Many laughed and made fun of him, and all obliged, due to the advanced age of the bus conductor. He again went to all the passengers, recollected all the roses filled with individual problems, and he asked the driver to stop the bus near the Hanuman temple. There he was, and he got down, offered the flowers to the deity, and prayed on behalf of all the passengers. This action of the conductor was usual on Indian roads.

Everyone was surprised by the good gestures of this conductor. He firmly believed that for him, if not for many on the bus, the problem would be resolved, and he strongly believed that Lord Hanuman was a deity who listened to all genuine problems and gave solutions. Many in the bus felt at ease, just as Madhav and Mahati felt very happy as if they had passed IITJEE, and this simple act of good gesture by the conductor made a difference to many in the bus. This experience made Mahati feel as if she were on cloud 9.

All without exception, she thanked the conductor and paid that lady with flowers, a minimum of Rs ten and several much more, and a few purchased more flowers. Never in her life could she sell so many flowers in a bus. She was extremely happy, as she could return home early and also purchase a gift for her son.

The bus conductor was a real hero; this incident got etched in the hearts of many, and Madhav decided on that day that he would try his best to bring some happiness to someone's face. Mahati felt that the purpose of life was not to earn more, lead a luxurious life, have many international trips, and eat luxurious food, but to bring joy into others' lives, and this small incident transformed her life forever. No one knows how love blossoms between two individuals, and sometimes a few events like this act as a spark to ignite this passion called love.

This particular incident has sparked an attraction in Mahati towards Madhav. But Madhav was of the opinion that Mahati was close to Bhavin, and in view of this, Madhav was always keeping away from Mahati and was only interacting at times when required.

The initiation of an attraction may be several times accidental due to several factors, and Mahati developed a strong feeling towards Madhav. In view of this, she was visiting Madhav at his place for more clarification in math and physics. She was also, at times, warning Madhav to give equal importance to chemistry.

Madhav also developed a feeling of comfort when Mahati was near, and he wanted to spend more time together. Initially, it all starts to meet often, and after some time, you feel a mild touch with a pretext of helping and finally appreciating her. These are all the vibrations that one experiences in love. This slowly moves and engulfs the system, and nothing will be seen later, which is why love is not only blind but also impulsive and makes the emotions uncontrolled.

In spite of a very strong urge, Madhav never made any advancements, expressed his affection for Mahati, and always maintained a dignified distance and showed maturity. This is necessary at that stage, as studying and passing IITJEE was more important than this attraction.

The Visit to Lord Shiva's Temple

It was a usual Saturday evening, and Madhav prepared to visit the Lord Sivas temple about four kilometres from their rooms in the evening. This has been the usual practice, and Madhav never missed his visit to the temple on Saturday evening. This is in spite of the fact that the next day there was an exam or any other class. No one really understood this behaviour, and boys of his age group refused to visit the temple or any other religious places as systematically as Madhav did.

When Madhav opened his room and was about to leave and move out, he saw Mahati, dressed in a typical, traditional Selwarkamez and matching dupatta. The colour of the salwar kameez was light golden yellow with orange borders, and the dupatta was fairly dark orange. She has combed her long and smooth hair, allowed it to flow down, let it loose, and tied it with an orange band at the end. Madhav never noticed girls looking so beautiful, and he could not turn away his eyes from Mahati. She was looking so stunning. The colour of the dress, her simple but elegant hairstyle, and her dressing style looked simple but very charming. No one knows how or why girls look so beautiful and attractive.

Mahati smiled at Madhav and tried to initiate conservation. Madhav resisted his best to avoid her, as she might be a nuisance during his visit to the temple. In addition, walking with her all the way to the temple and returning may attract the attention of his friends, and he wanted to avoid it and tried to move away, just pretending to ignore Mahati.

Mahati said, "Madhav, can I join you for your visit to the temple?"

Now it was impossible to say no, and he said that he was visiting Siva Temple, which is about 4 km away, and she might find it difficult to walk such large distances. With tomorrow being an important exam, was she really interested in visiting the temple instead of studying?

She could take an auto if she still wanted to visit, and he could meet her there if possible.

At this stage, Mahati replied, "I think I can walk, and I have made all the preparations for tomorrow's exams. I am looking forward to this visit to the temple in the morning. I am capable of walking 10 km faster than you, and I was at my best in my sports, so there is no issue. If you feel uncomfortable walking with me, then I will make my own way to reach the temple, and I have checked on Google how to reach there."

At this stage, Madhav was embarrassed and had no reply, and he said you could reach the temple and he would reach it later. There was not much argument to make. In addition, he had to visit a nearby shop to purchase fruits and pooja material, and it might take some time before Mahati could proceed.

Now, Mahati has understood, and she said, "Madhav, you may know, it is not that safe for girls to walk alone. Please complete the purchase of pooja material and come down, and we can walk."

"My only condition is that you please come down the lane at the end of the road, and I will bring an auto, and we will travel together, if this is acceptable to you:

"Fine," Madhav said, "I will join, and please make it as quickly as possible".

They both visited the temple, had the darshan of the lord, Madhav, had his usual three pradakshanas and chanted mantras for about 30 minutes, took prasadam, and very politely initiated conversation with the priest and inquired about his son's age. He also introduced Mahati as his classmate and took the priest's blessings.

At this stage, Mahati asked Madhav why he visits temples; does he believe that the Lord Siva will bless him so that he can pass his exam? It is just an act of bribery to the Lord, and she has never approved of this. Madhav maintained an absolute silence and just smiled away and kept quiet.

At this stage, Mahati felt that she had an upper hand over Madhav, which she never had in her studies.

Mahati said just to test and irritate Madhav, "This superstitious behaviour as to why we are having so many scrupulous Sadhus and Ashrams and they are all looting the public in the name of the Lord, and the Lord is just a stone and helps only those who want to make money using the God in the temples. This is the worst form of slavery and a mean way of showing devotion to the Lord. Does God actually help or protect anyone, and what is the very purpose of God in the midst of the current busy world? According to me, it is just a waste of time, and may the mighty win without any support from God.

Mahati knows fully well that she has touched an emotional chord and exposed Madhav and his devotion to the Lord, and this act of visiting temples is to pretend to prove and impress the girls and nothing more. For all this, Madhav was highly receptive and continued to keep silent.

Finally, Mahati said, "It is the upbringing in an orthodox family that has brought in all ills to society?

At this stage, Madhav thought that keeping silence would cost him much and that he should answer and state his point of view, not with the intention of convincing. If a person has made up his mind and is not willing to listen to other points of view to know the truth, the only way to move forward is to tell their point of view with no intention to convince. Often, an argument between two people is an exchange of ignorance rather than intelligence.

For many of us, the Lord exists as our firm belief. His existence is a function of our difficulty level at a given time. If things are going well in your life, your belief in the Lord keeps on increasing, and if you face serious problems, your belief comes down to the Lord. The moment the problems are sorted and you attribute them by force to the actions of the Lord, your confidence in the Lord increases. Imagine a straight line from zero to 100, people who do not believe in the Lord at any time in their lives under all circumstances are called atheists, and people who, at the point 100 (maximum), believe that their belief in the Lord is not a function of difficulties and that they have an unshakeable belief in the Lord. Most of us are somewhere between 0 and 100 and must try to be close to 100. This means you accept both difficulties and pleasures with equanimity and ask the Lord to give you the mental strength to face the sorrow, pain, and other problems without too much disturbance and also not get too elated when success arrives.

After the initial description of the Lord according to him, Madhav continued,

"Mahati, I am simple at heart, rational, and fully aware that I will do whatever I am fully convinced of. I am a science student, and logic and reasoning are hallmarks of any thought process. Do not feel offended, and now I will give you some thought, and at no stage will I ask you to agree with my point of view but prove me wrong after enough thought process that is logical. In my view, you are very naïve and ignorant of facts, and at the same time, with your half-knowledge, try to express your point in the most unconvincing manner, even to yourself. This is the language of a person who is not reasonable in his or her own logic."

Mahati was stunned at the depth of his knowledge and just kept silent, curious to know more.

The priest's son, Siddhanth, had failed IITJEE twice and had moved for his studies elsewhere. The priest is always close to the Lord, and his own objective in life is to serve the Lord with the utmost devotion. If priest sons have not qualified, how can anyone be sure of the prayers offered to Lord Siva to bless them to pass any exam? Forget about the IITJEE.

Now, imagine all students from the X10 batch visiting the Lord Sivas temple daily and praying intensively, and none of the students from the X1 batch visiting the temple even once. Do you think the X10 students will pass the exams? In my view, if you conduct this experiment, none of X10 will pass. Did the Lord Siva ask any of the students to come and pray so that He could pass them? It is a self-defeating exercise to do this activity, and you decided to do it unilaterally, except for Lord Siva to help you, and you call this act bribery. Never visit a temple or any religious place with selfish intent.

The three great religious people the world knows who moved in flesh and blood had their own stories, and people made them gods for their own reasons.

Take, for example, Adi Sankaracharya, an exponent in Indian philosophy who has written more than 300 books considered the texts of Advaitha philosophy and savvier of Hindu religion, belonged to 500 BC, travelled across India several times, and established four mutts existing even today. He died at the age of thirty-two. He opted to be separated from his mother and attended to her at the end of her life and performed her last rights. A brief look at his life shows he had his own ups and downs. Did he not pray to Lord Siva to have a comfortable life, be with his mother, and serve her when she wanted him the most? He chose to lead life in his own way for the betterment of society, and he never asked for anything for himself. At best, he might have asked him to give him strength to help society, and his teachings are more relevant now as well. He did not ask Lord Siva for anything for his own selfish interests, nor did the Lord grant anything; he was committed to doing what he felt was right through continuous action, just by visiting temples and studying scriptures. The Lord may not grant what anyone wants.

Take the example of Swami Ramana Maharashi, who had a near-death experience at the age of 16 and then had the realisation. Maharshi died in 1950. If you happen to visit Annamalai, many devotees feel his presence there even now. We just think that the Lord should have kept his suffering to a minimum and liberated him early. This is our and devotees' wish, but not from the Sri Ramana Maharshi; he was not attached to the body, and he had spent his final years in a small room and left profound impressions of his own teachings, which are seen and felt even now.

If the Lord Shiva was so easily accessible to all and fulfilled promises just by visiting temples, then the human story would have been different.

Please tell me how I can bribe the Lord and make me pass my exams; in fact, I am not a devotee of that magnitude.

Take the example of Swami Vivekananda; he had more than thirty health issues, died at the age of 39, and achieved so much that he is remembered even today for his lectures and writings. He had so many health issues and suffered, but continued. He was an ardent devotee of the goddess Durga, and she should have given him a healthy and long life so that he could continue to contribute to society.

When so many luminaires and great devotees had suffered and gone through many difficult times and many ups and downs in life, if it could have been easy, they could have prayed to the Lord Siva to help them transform society. I have taken the examples of the people who are no more, and now there are several devotees alive who are constantly at the lotus feet of the Lord and continue to go through life struggles. How do you expect that I can ask Lord Siva to pass me IITJEE by just visiting His temple?

I would like to give you a rather simple and more relevant example, which is current. Our family regularly visits Lord Balaji at Tirupati. From there, we claim about 3600 steps to reach the top of the hill called Tirumala. It takes about 3 to 4 hours for a healthy person. Generally, you have to book in advance and pay Rs 300 online to get entry to the queue. It takes about 2 to 3 hours for the darshan of the Lord. That experience is mesmerising, and having the darshan of the Lord even for a few seconds, you tend to forget all the problems and pray to the Lord and have eye-to eye communication from the Lord to express your wishes. Granting is the Lord's prerogative.

Now, you imagine that on average, about 50,000 to 80,000 devotees may be visiting the Lord daily. They have darshan and offload their problems at the lotus feet of the Lord, have a prasadam, and exit from the temple. I watched for hours at the exit gate, and I have seen from the exit gate for hours. In fact, all devotees seem to be fully satisfied, content, and peaceful after the darshan; I have not found even a single devotee upset after the darshan of the Lord. I was wondering how the Lord fulfilled all the wishes of devotees. Most of the devotees take extreme pain to travel to Tirumala and stand in the queue and wait for hours to have darsan, and that too for a few seconds. They feel content that all their hardships were worth their darshan. This is a fact and is called a belief. It is strongly believed that after darshan for many, the subconscious mind imagines successes, leading to improved effort, which in turn realises success.

To illustrate, I will tell you a small story that appeared in a children's magazine about 10 years ago.

There was an astrologer in a remote village somewhere in south India. He was consulted by the kings and many people who were famous, and there was a strong belief that his predictions were right, and no one found fault with his predictions. He could also predict the gender of a baby born just before delivery. Many couples used to visit him, and most of the time, his predictions were right. He used to enter in a log book and maintain these books for years. He was making his calculations to the best of his ability, and he was also not charging anything for his services. Whatever was offered, he was using these funds to feed students who were studying in his ashram. The trick was that in the log book, he wrote the opposite gender of what he said for the couple; if he had said female for a particular couple, in the book he was writing male. Even if predictions go wrong for any reason, it is a prediction, which may sometimes go wrong. When the couple visits him about his wrong predictions, he will show that his prediction was right, the parents have heard wrong, and his predictions are right. There was no way to prove he was wrong.

Last time, I was climbing the Tirumala, and I met several devotees who were climbing along with me in the hot sun. Let me tell you about two cases.

A young couple from the US were visiting Tirumala to have darshan of the Lord along with their blind son. They had tried their best to provide all the facilities that they could get in the US but could not get the vision of their own son, as his optic nerve was damaged. On another occasion, a father from a remote part of Rajasthan was climbing with his daughter, who looked so cute but had severe autism, and he had no place to go anywhere in the world but to fall at the feet of the lotus feet of the lord. Now, miracles might happen, and something good will happen, and hope is the driving force behind living. Lord will not be selective and give His helping hand to all at His mercy, but He will definitely give you strength to handle the realities that might occur against our wishes.

You may ask Mahati, then why do I regularly visit this temple, which is built of a concrete wall and a stone in the form of Linga, called Siva, fully knowing that the Lord will not help me? Am I just wasting my time and energy?

Now I will tell you my answer, and if you are rational enough, you will be convinced.

At that moment, Mahati was lost, speechless, and bewildered. How can a boy of less than 20 years of age be so learned and present arguments that any rational and ordinary mind like mine can comprehend? Mahati was looking for the next answers.

“Most of the people come to the temple out of fear for the Lord. Since childhood, we have seen pictures in the temples, torturing people who commit sin in hell. This helps devotees avoid committing sins, and many visit the Lord out of fear. This is a general practice for many.

Another section of people visit the temple more out of desire or to fulfil their genuine or not-so-genuine demands and desires, just as you have mentioned. I do not think this is the best reason to visit the temple, but there is nothing wrong with it. Generally, if it is fulfilled, the devotee will think it is due to the Lord's grant, and if it is not fulfilled, the devotee thinks he may not deserve this. No one gets angry at the Lord, as the Lord is not available for any interrogation.

The next set of people visit the temple to show their gratitude to the Lord because He has given them several things, and He may not ask for anything in return. In addition, a few are conditioned to think that the Lord has given us the air we breathe, the light of the Sun, and, finally, the entire world. They should show their gratitude and thank the Lord. This is definitely a better option as there is no expectation from the Lord. These people accept what is in their way and move on in life.

Finally, few people visit the Lord because they love Him. These are very special and have moved a step further, loving the Lord unconditionally. They firmly believe that whatever happens is the wish of the Lord, and they continue to do their duty without any expectation. In my opinion, they are the best and may fine-tune their lives with minimum wants. This set of people is not easy to find.

I first come to the temple to offer my prayers in the form of gratitude for all the things Lord Siva has given me in life so far. I am healthy, educated, and I have some funds to retake the IITJEE exam for the second time. There are thousands who are more hardworking than I am but do not have the necessary finances to come here and study. This is a fact. I have no statistics, but my own friend has joined an engineering college near Mumbai, and he was so happy, and he would do well. I keep visiting the Tata Memorial Centre (TMC) for some service quite often at a nearby place, and I see how fortunate I am to be alive and not undergo suffering. Next time when you are back at IITB, please visit TMC, and you can feel the suffering. You will also visit the temple just to show your gratitude to the Lord. Not many are sensitive, but I am, and this is how my family upbringing has taught me. You may not feel and may not experience the grace of the Lord and assume all things are granted more as your right and try your best to be insensitive to all that is there and given to you.

I visit a temple for its serenity, calmness, bhajans, Vedic chants, and to meet good people who visit the temple very frequently. I like to sing the Lord's name, and this singing gives me inner strength. This has been taught to me since my childhood. Now, the real reason for praying is to grant me the mental strength to give my best and to accept the end result of the IITJEE. Even if I pass or fail, I should have the strength to accept the end result to the Lord. On that day when the result comes, I should sleep for seven hours without any disturbance. This is possible only by having a person I call the Lord, who holds me through my best and worst times. By visiting temples, I get positivity in my body and become activated, as I am convinced that I am doing what is right, and I am not asking for anything from the Lord.

Mahati, please also understand, we cannot choose our parents, siblings, intelligence, birth, death, or even health. The only thing in our hands is hard work, commitment, and, above all, giving our best towards what we do. This is what you get by visiting a temple. For me, it might be something else for you, but the least we get is to take the right direction and evolve as a person who is sensitive and concerned. I have no other wish when I visit the temple, and I have seen this happening to me every time I get back home. I feel energised and more focused. This may or may not affect my IITJEE results.

I would like to tell you a small story. There was an old lady. After the death of her husband, she was begging as she could not work for her daily living. An elderly man gave her Rs 1000 and food and asked her why she was begging, as her son, whom he met recently, was earning well. He also said that he kept on sending enough money to his mother every month. But the old lady was surprised and she said she received a small colourful sheet that she could not read. She kept it in a safe place as a memory of her son. It was, in fact, a cheque for a substantial amount that could take care of all the needs of this old lady. Now, all of us are like this. We do not know the values, nor are we interested in reading, knowing, or exploring ourselves to find out what it is. We are just like that old lady, intelligent but ignorant people, we keep on doubting without exploring.

"At this stage, it is necessary to understand the following two important proverbs," says Madhav, "'Lord's actions are inscrutable' and 'Lord helps those who help themselves.'"

This does not mean that you get everything only by your own efforts; the Lord's intervention is always here. Surrendering to the Lord after offering the end result, positive or negative, without questioning, gives you immense satisfaction, says Madhav. In fact, this helps several, like me, as most of the time is wasted thinking about the imminent failure.

Faith in the Lord is to accept Him without any expectations, is the rule rather than the exception for a selected few. It takes time to accept this fact for many. It is important to mention that action and doing a good job are only in our hands. This is the only way to wipe out all our difficulties and sufferings. The Lord will give you the strength to do this action and also give you the strength to accept the results of this action, whether good or bad.

There are two kinds of people in the world. a) I have seen and explored, and only 1% of people belong to the category who have had the tenacity to explore, and b) I have also seen are the people who follow in the footsteps of the 99% who belong to the category.

My great-grandfather and my grandfathers were school teachers in a village school. They lived their lives very happily and lived content and fulfilling lives. They always did all that was possible and left the final course to be decided by Lord Siva. My father, in spite of all extreme difficulties in life, was always happy, even at the lowest points in his life. He followed the same principle of his elders, and I also belong to that 99% of people who follow the teachings of the people who have shown us the direction. You have to be extremely tough to be in that 1%

category, to explore and convince from the start to the end by yourself, and it's not an easy task by any means.

Finally, I would like to add that none of us are happy all the time. There are good times and bad times, and they will pass by like waves in an ocean. However, when you have extreme pain and extreme difficulty, you cannot handle it on your own. You can fall back on Lord Siva to give you a helping hand and tide over the current problem or give you enough courage to accept the problem and move on in life. Similarly, extreme happiness brings in pain subsequently, and this has to be controlled. The maintenance of equanimity and balance, which can be handled by any person to himself, needs divine interventions.

I always tried my best to be happy like my elders and follow their path, not blindly, but giving it my best to explore and question.

"Sorry for indirectly calling you a 'pseudo-rationalist,'" said Madhav, mildly.

Now it was close to 8.30 pm, and Mahati did not feel the passage of time. It looked as if time was frozen. For the first time, she had realised that each and every question had been answered unambiguously, and there was no need for further argument.

Madhav said, "Now it is close to 8.30 pm. If we delay, we may not get an auto. Please, let us rush back, and you can get down to your room. On the way, drop me near the market."

At that stage, Mahati came to her senses and realised that Madhav did not want to come in the same auto up to the apartment to avoid embarrassment for her. Her respect towards Madhav grew multifold.

Mahati in Hospital

Days were rolling by, and the syllabus was almost coming to an end. In order to know and evaluate, the coaching centres kept conducting model test papers for almost the entire syllabus. Generally, the question papers were fairly difficult, and the difficulty level was even tougher than that actually asked in IITJEE. This was to make students lose their confidence a bit at this stage and work hard, thinking about their relatively bad performance in the first model test exams.

The preparations for this test series were very demanding for students, and all wanted to compete to the best of their ability. In the minds of most students, X1 and X2 students always wanted to keep their performance above other batches, and X3 students always wanted to do better than X1 students. This competition was very demanding.

These tests made many students restless and sometimes deprived them of sleep, which had a bearing on their overall health.

Mahati developed severe pain in the abdomen with high fever and mild dehydration around 1:00 a.m. Most of the students were studying at that time, and Mahati initially wanted to call Bhavin as he had a smart lady cook who was quite friendly with Mahati. Although Mahati also had a cook, she was very naïve and not educated and was not in a position to understand situations and needs very quickly. Bhavin could not receive the phone call as he had already fallen asleep and was fully tired. Then she called Madhav and explained her condition. Madhav immediately rushed to Mahati's room, gave her some water, and then rushed to get an auto. Madhav was fully aware of the nearby excellent hospital and its location. Before going to fetch an auto, Madhav thought that it was his duty to inform Bhavin, so he woke up Bhavin and informed him of the urgent need to take Mahati to the hospital, then rushed down to get an auto.

Mahati's condition became worse, and it was not possible for her to climb down. She had to be carried in a thicker bedsheet by four students, and by that time, the house owner also started to help them. By the time the auto arrived, all had placed Mahati in the auto along with her cook, and Madhav volunteered to go to the hospital. He shared the front seat with the driver as there was no place in the back. He asked the others to take another auto and accompany them to the Kota Hospital, as this would help speed up the process.

Bhavin and other friends never wanted to go, as the exams were nearing, and going to the hospital may ruin their preparation. Madhav was capable and could handle the situation, and if required, he could call for help, so thinking, they resumed their activities. There is a difference in the way people react to situations, and this is mostly guided by their upbringing.

Madhav was expecting another auto to come, as he was finding it difficult to handle the situation, and he didn't have much money left for the preliminary admission process.

However, after reaching the hospital, he rushed to get a stretcher and alerted the local resident doctor. Mahati was too weak to notice anything. Madhav paid the initial admission fee and purchased medicines, waiting outside for the main doctor to come. Madhav was more worried about Mahati's health than the model test to be held the next day.

It took almost three days for Mahati to speak and start taking a liquid diet. When Mahati opened her eyes, her mother, father, and uncle were all present, and the best possible treatment was being given. Madhav was waiting outside and willing to return since their parents were there.

A day before, Madhav felt the need to inform Mahati's parents and ask them to come to the Kota hospital, and he considered this his responsibility.

The following conversation took place between Madhav and Mahati on the second day of her hospitalisation:

"Mahati, can you please share your parents' mobile number, I would like to inform them?" Madhav said.

Mahati was pretty weak and warned Madhav not to inform her parents as they were not aware of her present stay in Kota, and if they came, she might not continue her studies there.

"Mahati, it is important that I tell your parents, and even if it results in you leaving Kota if they come to know through someone else or if the treatment is not what it should be, then this might be a cause for serious concern. I am not prepared for this under any circumstances. In case your parents take you against your wishes, I will protect you at all costs, take care of you, and ensure that you write your IITJEE exams as per your choice."

Speaking in a fairly loud voice, Madhav took Mahati's phone and forced her to open it. He then called her mother.

At that moment, Mahati hated Madhav. She was staying against the wishes of her own parents. This action of Madhav was not acceptable to her, and she could not help as she was too weak to fight. She also needed the help of Madhav, as no one was there around.

The Madhav's relationship with his parents was fine, and he could not understand that a relationship between a daughter and her parents could be so bad that she could come and stay at an unknown place without the consent of her own parents. This was a real concern.

Mahati returned to her room and started to prepare, and her mother stayed back for some time till Mahati felt better. This time, Mahati was staying with the consent of her mother, though half-heartedly. She was happy for her, though her mother gave permission to her quite reluctantly.

Mahati was very grateful for Madhav's good gesture of involving her parents when she was sick. Though she felt bad at that time, her liking for Madhav grew greatly. At the same time, Bhavin's selfish nature was exposed. Though Mahati never expressed herself openly, she made up her mind and directed her attention elsewhere and never opened her heart. Madhav never felt the need to open this topic again and felt closer to Mahati when he was at the hospital nursing her throughout the night.

Inner Strength

It was Saturday, and Madhav, as usual, had plans to visit the Lord Siva temple. However, for his X3 batch, there was a first preliminary examination covering the whole syllabus from 4:00 p.m. to 7:00 p.m., and Madhav could hardly miss this. Madhav decided that he would write the exam, and then he would reach the temple complex directly from the examination centre, as this would give him a sense of comfort. He was sure he would miss the Arati scheduled at 7:30 p.m., but he would have the darshan of the lord.

As Madhav was going to the examination hall at 4:00 p.m., he saw both Mahati and Bhavin returning in a jubilant mood, indicating a possible good performance. In general, students' happiness is worth watching when they perform well in an exam, and this is reflected on their faces. Both Mahati and Bhavin did not notice Madhav, but Madhav knew that Bhavin had noticed him walking towards the examination centre and pretended as if he had not. Bhavin's only intention was that Mahati should not wish him and start a small conversation. Sometimes Bhavin was overprotective towards Mahati. In addition, they were planning to go to a nearby hotel in the evening to celebrate their good performance in the exam. Bhavin was not keen on visiting temples, and he always believed that self-help was the best, which was not entirely wrong. In addition, Bhavin had some faint idea that Mahati was not in her room for most of the Saturdays during the evening, but he was not fully aware that Mahati, along with Madhav, were visiting the temples.

Madhav did quite well in Physics and Mathematics and, for a change, did fairly well in chemistry.

After the examination, Madhav reached the Siva temple just after the completion of ARATI, and after prasadam, he decided to sit in the garden. To his surprise, he found Mahati sitting there and waiting for Madhav to join her. Mahati informed Madhav that she was not keen on going to dinner with Bhavin and his friends from the X1 batch, as she was not feeling well and wanted to spend more time at the temple. Mahati was quite aware that Bhavin had not extended that invitation, as Madhav was from the X3 batch. Sometimes, knowingly, we underestimate others to boost our confidence level, and this is how most human beings are built.

As usual, the conversation started, and Mahati was very impressed with the earlier discussion at the temple. She wanted to delve a bit deeper and also wanted to know if there were general problems we faced and if solace could be found at temples. This was a difficult and general question, and there is no simple answer to it. She thought that Madhav would keep quiet and express his inability to answer.

Contrary to Mahati's view, Madhav started off with specifics.

"Most of us believe that all of us should do well and be in a state of happiness. And to achieve this, we all involve ourselves both intellectually, emotionally, and physically and struggle day by day to achieve some happiness. Many times we may feel content and happy, but the next day something hard strikes and we are highly disappointed, and the cycle goes on and on. For many, eternal happiness is always eluding, and the more one runs after, the faster happiness runs, finally, if one does not get the happiness one deserves, one now blames all, including oneself.

The most important quality of happy living is to maintain a good relationship with your family, relatives, and friends, and that is possible by showering love and affection from the heart with practically no expectations or strings attached. It is absolutely important that you be affectionate and lovable. However, too much attachment drives negative emotions, which may bring sorrow and unhappiness. The moment you have some expectations, there is a possibility that you are disappointed, as we have control over others."

At this stage, Mahati felt lost, and she realised that the health issues that her father was suffering were due to excessive attachment and, in turn, too many things, that may not be realised. Mahati felt she should have obliged her parents instead of going through the current grill at Kota. For a moment, she felt sorry for herself but immediately realised that she had the freedom to do what she liked. It is the responsibility of parents to allow children to realise their dreams instead of pushing their personal agenda. This appeared very harsh on her, but she found nowhere to go except to keep quiet.

"Mahati, you seem lost." says Madhav gently.

The next aspect to be considered is being healthy, both physically and mentally. In fact, good mental health leads to good physical health.

The physical health of an individual depends on several factors, including the genetic history of the family, quality of life, food and exercise, one's attitudes and routines, and finally, the commitment to keep oneself healthy. This has been discussed very extensively, and many of us know it well. My only concept of physical health is to maintain a balanced weight by eating moderately, experiencing no pain in any part of the body, getting good uninterrupted sleep for 7 to 8 hours, and having good bowel movements.

I will just narrate a small incident that happened in our family last year. A friend of my father was invited to dinner at my place, and we all observed that he was a very moderate eater. At the end of the dinner, I offered him ice cream with gulab jamon. He was reluctant to accept, and I had to force him to accept, in my opinion, I was doing my duty as a good host. He has agreed on one condition: I should accompany him after dinner for a walk. I had agreed. I was about to go to sleep when the guest knocked at my door and asked me to keep my promise. I had no option but to oblige. He walked from night 10.30 pm to early morning 2.00 am the next day to burn the extra calories he had eaten, especially the ice cream with gulab jamun. From that day until today, I have never forced anyone to take any extra leave-alone, sweets. Our guest has ensured that he has burned all the extra fat he has taken during the dinner so that his weight does not increase. Many are extremely cautious and disciplined and maintain strict control over their weight.

Everything in moderation is essential for good physical health. If you, for some reason, eat something that is not suitable but take it just for taste, it will disturb your bowel movement. It is not easy to prescribe a general rule for food intake, and individuals have to fine-tune so that they are energetic and healthy from start to finish. The other most important thing is to support all parts of the body, especially the brain, which is always immersed in different fluids, including blood. I presume a minuscule amount of this food is also responsible for the functioning of the mind and, in some way, is responsible for our mental health.

Before we move on to mental health, let me have some comments on bowel movements. Nowadays, most of us have Western-type washrooms, which have become fashionable and are not suitable for the digestion of Indian food. In fact, in many flats, Indian-type washrooms are not available, and one is forced to use the existing western washrooms. The trick is to mimic the bowel movement by squatting on the floor, and then moving on to the Western washrooms. This I had learned from a priest when we visited a temple deep in the south, and this is what I practice and never complain about the absence of Indian-type washrooms. This may look ridiculous and silly, but according to me, it is absolutely necessary for good physical health.

Now, let us move on to mental health. According to doctors, mental health causes more than 80% of health-related issues, and this is a very serious issue that many do not know and do not consider necessary to learn. There are several negative and positive emotions, and the negative emotions that have a very strong effect on the quality of life and health are anger, jealousy, hatred, and arrogance. Each of these negative emotions will trigger a sense of pulse in our system, eventually becoming a habit and leading to several health-related issues. It may appear that these emotions do not disturb us in the beginning, but eventually, they may have far-reaching consequences later. Momentarily, you may feel good and have a sense of self-gratification, and in the long run, as these qualities become habits, they may cause irreversible damage to the system.

Now the question is how to overcome these emotions and what, how, and who controls them. The solution for me exists in visiting temples as we feel our minds are grounded.

Imagine a chariot that was used as a vehicle during the earlier wars. There are four systems in this chariot: the person who is sitting in the chariot is yourself; the charioteer who is riding the chariot; the horses, who are pulling the chariot; and finally, the reins, which control the horses by the charioteer. All these systems should function well and coherently for you to reach your destination. Imagine that if the charioteer wants to cause trouble, he may let loose the horses and apparently create momentary fear for the person travelling. If you have gone to any hill station, it may be Matheran, near Mumbai, and you hire a horse for a local trip. The horses are well trained, and they keep moving at the edge of the movement, and you feel dead-scared. If you look down for a moment, you see a very deep valley, and with any slip or step by the horse, you may tumble into the deep valley with no point of return.

Now, taking this analogy to our own system, you are travelling; the charioteer is the intelligence in you; the reins are the mind; and the horses are the body, the physical body. Now in the chariot, all are separate, but all of them are present in us together, and you cannot separate them at any point in time as these are deep inside your body. Now your negative emotions are in the framework of the mind, and controlling them is not easy. This is because, instead of you controlling these emotions, the mind controls them. Now the mind can be at times your friend and at times your own enemy. All problems arise due to a lack of control.

Imagine the worst form of emotion: anger. When you are angry, some chemical elements are formed in the brain, which have a bad effect on the body, and this emotion, anger, increases your breath and disturbs the power of thinking and understanding of the person at times, which eventually leads to excessive stress in the system.

Many of us want to practice a very disciplined life and force ourselves to follow it very meticulously. Whether it is getting up early, finishing an important assignment in a given period of time, or reducing the unwanted cravings for a particular form of food, the mind cheats you openly in front of you on the pretext of self-pity. The mind distracts by constantly oscillating between the past, future, and present, taking you to places and creating emotions that you never wanted. Imagine you wanted to study; immediately a memory comes in by the spell of the mind, and you are in the football match, and generally, it moves so fast that this control makes it difficult to concentrate for more than 10 to 15 minutes, and beyond that, there will be distractions.

Then how do you control and do only those things that you want to do?

"This is not an easy task even for the best of people, and for me, visiting temples helps and keeps me grounded. There are many other options, like meditation, chanting a mantra, the habit of giving or charity, showing a sense of gratitude for all that you have received from nature and trying your best to live in the present, listening to good music, etc., and it is for individuals to explore and practice very rigorously. It is easier said than done, but you have no other option than to constantly practice to get control over your mind. Imagine that there may be several surgeons who get the necessary expertise and are close to perfection only through constant practice, as well as musicians, dancers, and artists. Many have tried their best, and this path is quite touchy. This control of the mind is worth this exercise, as it will substantially reduce your negative emotions, increase your positive emotions, and control your mental health. These practices will help you to improve your physical and mental health, and these are vital to succeeding in any examination, and IITJEE is no exception."

As usual, it was time to return, and Mahati was convinced that, for the first time, she had learned something new and decided to take these learnings seriously. She just remembered her father and felt bad; she felt like flying to meet him. We all have a part to play in this complex world, and nature is the best teacher. The Lord is always there, if you believe in Him, who is kind and willing to help only those who ask for it genuinely. The only thing that is in our hands is to take action continuously; this is the only way of reducing suffering, pain, and sorrow while at the same time enhancing our productivity. Visiting temples provides you with an opportunity to ask for what you need, and granting is at the mercy of the Lord. However, He will provide the necessary inner strength to cope with the difficulties and suffering.

Finally, I would like to conclude that for every action there is a reaction, and for all negative emotions, especially hatred, jealousy, and ego, that is deeply rooted, manifest themselves at some stage, and cause an emotional imbalance that may result in both physical and mental health, which may be worse than death.

The important positive emotions is to be kind, hospitable, pleasant, understanding, forgiving, and many more are not easy to adapt; this has to be taught to the children by their parents and consciously developed by students for their own good till they become their habits instead of negative emotions.

The basic guidelines for healthy living are to always think good, say good, and act well, and there is very limited scope for any negative emotions in our system.

For a change, Mahati suggested to Madhav that they walk, as the weather was pleasant. Reluctantly, Madhav agreed, as it was getting slightly dark, it was a new place, and there were no street lights. As they were walking, near a turning point, a well-built man in his thirties suddenly appeared with a small knife and demanded something from Mahati. Mahati believed that wearing golden bangles to the temples would bring good luck. Both Mahati and Madhav were so scared, and even before Madhav could react, Mahati removed the bangles and was about to hand them over to the robber (thief). In a flash of a second, Madhav overpowered the robber and hit him hard in the stomach. Due to very quick action not anticipated by the robber, who made no resistance, he had no option but to run in the by-lanes and disappear in the darkness. Mahati was astonished and could not speak for minutes in shock. Madhav just gave her some water, returned the bangles to her to wear, and just started walking. The robber was no match for Madhav. For the first time, Mahati felt so safe to be with Madhav, and that incident was always in her memory. Mahati could see the power and body of Madhav, and her admiration increased. Madhav was a trained cricketer and also a black-belt karate player. He regularly did exercise in the evenings and yoga in the morning, and this was the reason for his courage to act when necessary. Mahati knew about the morning yoga practices but never thought that his strength and courage were so good that he could handle a well-built robber.

Final Test Series and Departure from Kota

The final test series was due next week, and there were only doubt-clearing sessions that too from 2:00 to 7:00 p.m. A few students always have doubts, and even on the day of the examination, they make their parents carry all the books and study till the start of the exams. In fact, most of these exams test concepts rather than memory and, many times, speed and accuracy. There is no need to read till the end and also burn the midnight oil. The most important point is to have a good sleep before the examination. This will give students enough rest, and this will help them solve numerical problems very efficiently. Studying from the start may provide self-satisfaction but may not be beneficial. Some students do not want to understand, and it is better to leave those to their fate.

This difficulty level of the final test was generally kept at the same level as IITJEE to keep the confidence level very high for students. This is to increase the confidence of the students just before the IITJEE. The coaching centre knew the physiology of the students, fine-tuned in favour of them, and tried their best to optimise their performance. The coaching institutes, after evaluating the final test papers, were fully aware of the number of students who were likely to pass and the number who were likely to come in the top 100 ranks. This is shown as the strength of the coaching colleges, and even IITs boast that a large number of top 100 students have joined a particular IIT. This also shows the quality of instruction, infrastructure, and placements at a given IIT.

On the day of the exams, as usual, students are very stressed and have reached the examination centre an hour before. Mahati and Bhavin reached the examination centre close to their residence, and Madhav had to go 6 km away. In any case, several students performed well, and so did Madhav, who had put in considerable effort to study chemistry towards the end; however, he could not get the concepts right, and this deficiency remained, and he could not get interested in that subject in spite of his hard work.

The ranks and the marks were available on the net, and the efficiency of these institutes was so high that they corrected all the papers and displayed the overall ranks and individual subject ranks and marks in each subject just 24 hours after the examination. In fact, the teaching staff, the staff who are involved in setting the question papers, and finally, the staff who are allowed to correct are all different and do not interact. This helps the management make a fairly good assessment of the teaching staff. Bhavin got 120th rank, Mahati got 1800th rank, and Madhav got a rank close to 3000. However, he was in the top 50 in physics and the top 40 in mathematics, and his rank was very bad in chemistry. As passing in each subject was essential, he got a rank as he just scraped through. There was a call from the principal for Madhav to meet him, and the institute and principal said there would be separate coaching for him in chemistry, as he had a chance of getting a top 100 rank, Madhav knew that just teaching would not develop. He politely refused special classes and said that he would work hard as there are still 28 days until the actual IITJEE examination. Few students change, and their system is built accordingly. Neither Madhav nor his parents were very concerned, but they never expressed their thoughts and expectations to Madhav.

Finally, the day had come, all had bid farewell, and it was time to depart. Madhav went first to Bhavin to wish him the best, and Bhavin's response was very cold. He was of the opinion that if Madhav studied well in the remaining 20 days of chemistry, there was the possibility that Madhav may get a better rank than him, and this was not acceptable to him.

Madhav then went to Mahati and bid her bye, and he could see that her moist eyes could not understand. Mahati and Bhavin's parents were there and had arranged for a car to Jaipur and, from there, a plane to Mumbai. Madhav's father could not come due to his own commitments, so he decided to go by train, and finally, all of them bade good-bye with a promise to meet sometime later as dictated by Providence. Madhav was deeply emotional as his father did not come to Kota to take him back, and he was of the opinion that something was seriously wrong on the home front. Not even once did his mother visit him, and all the time, only his father visited him. His mother, Lakshmi, was talking to him at times, and could sense shrillness and pain in her voice, and he suspected something must be serious at his home. He just went to a lone place near the station and cried for hours with no one to console him; as always, he had to console himself.

Sometimes, times Lord gives problems to those who are close to him as only they can handle such problems, and whether it is true or not, let us leave the individual to decide.

Chapter III

The Resilience

There are always struggles in life. Accepting all challenges gracefully to maintain equanimity to not be elated during happy moments and depressed during difficult times.

A balanced attitude towards demands is essential for a contented and peaceful career.

Uncertainties

Many things in life do not follow the principles of planning to near perfection. Like in war, all preparations and planes are made; the complete strength of the enemy is estimated and planned intensely. Help is taken from secret agents, and resources are utilised. We are of the opinion that victory is there, and we just have to grab it. Things can go wrong and may not follow the predicted lines. But you might have failed to gauge the strength of the enemy. It is normal to underestimate the inherent strength of the enemy army and make your own assumptions, but fail to recognise the fire or power to fight if pushed. For many, realisation comes at a time when things have precipitated. This must be the reason why wars take place, and many times an army that appears to be weak wins, and no amount of justification or logistics can explain the realities.

Similarly, nature has its own plans and destiny and takes you on a roller coaster ride. In most cases, many might have prepared for the worst so that when everything reveals itself in its most nascent form, but nature takes you to an unknown destination, you are not mentally prepared.

Madhav, Mahati, and Bhavin had their own preparations and made all that possible. They have invested one more year, taken the best coaching available at their disposal, invested time, faced the worst unnatural competition at the coaching institutes, and above all, their families have made several sacrifices and were willing to accept the uncertainties about the results. The worst, not qualified, was always there, dangling like a sword on their heads. There are lakhs of students who go through this path, and many think they deserve some success but do not realise that the efforts and sacrifices made by others are even greater. A family sold their property in a remote village to educate their younger brother at Kota. It is not possible to gauge the pressure and stress the system is loading on these young boys and girls, and many are not prepared, which, if unsuccessful, may result in events uncalled for. Finally, success or failure at an exam does not automatically construe as success, as in life there are many variants, and the young minds do not realise this.

Many students who have travelled this difficult path, given their best-seen failures, are prepared to face many problems in life and do not hesitate to take risks. This inner strength naturally develops called resilience, which is guaranteed to all who take up any exam with the utmost sincerity and seriousness. A big reward is waiting for you, and that makes you feel that the path you took was worth it, and so must failure. This lesson learned can be understood as an experience, and an individual must go through this experience; there are no shortcuts. Down the memory lane, passing or failure leaves no marks at all, and all feel that whatever has happened to them was the right thing to happen, and they show their gratitude to the system. Many thank the system for their failure, which made them look for other, even more rewarding professions. This mental preparedness to face challenges and cooperation from families is vital when students see failures.

Inner Voice

Madhav takes the late-evening train from Kota and arrives at Mumbai Central early in the morning the next day. As usual, the station was crowded with passengers arriving from many places. Madhav has heavy luggage, and he was expecting his father, Vishnu, to come to the station. In fact, Vishnu had not visited Madhav at Kota many times, like other parents. It is important that the boys and girls have confidence that they will do all that is necessary, and this will convey a sense of relief to the parents. Vishnu, on his part, knows that Madhav was trained to handle his problems and make the right decisions, and if some things went wrong, he was equipped to handle them on his own.

Now, Madhav, with all his difficulty, brings down his luggage and waits for his father. His father was not picking up the mobile, and this makes Madhav feel like crying and highly disheartened. Tears rolled down, and he felt helpless.

He called a local porter and took a taxi to reach his residence. The house was locked. The neighbours opened the house, handed over the keys, gave him tea and breakfast, and made him comfortable. Madhav was maintaining absolute silence and was expecting something was wrong, as no one was even smiling or uttering a word.

Finally, his father arrives and asks Madhav to prepare to go to his mother, who was admitted to the hospital. Now, Madhav could understand why his father was asking him to stay back in Kota and write the exams in Jaipur.

He just followed his father, and his mother was waiting to see Madhav. In a few seconds, Madhav could spend his time with his mother, and finally, after blessing him, she left for her heavenly abode. Madhav was devastated and was gaining strength to control his emotions. He could see tears in the eyes of his father and how he has handled it all single-handedly, taking care of and nursing his mother for more than six months. Madhav just hugged his father, which he never did in his whole life, and Madhav felt so much warmth and confidence to live. This hug was also reassuring to both that they had to be there for one another. The intensity of the pain of losing your parents was not easy to explain. Not much time was left to even grieve to one's heart's content; the exams were there, and he had to be attentive. Madhav has lost precious two weeks and, on the advice of his father, started to prepare and take the exams, which were to start in about ten days.

The Day of Examinations

This is not just another examination. Many want to ace it, and students have worked very hard to satisfy themselves that they are good and also make parents feel proud. This is, of course, apart from the benefits that they may reap after the completion of their course.

As too much was at stake, so was the pressure, and there was always a fear of not performing at the best. Many students fell sick or experienced blank and unexpected drowsiness, and this mental trauma bothers students as well as parents.

Today, the system allows students to choose a date for exams and also provides other flexibilities. The two-stage examinations allow students to drop off after the first stage, and only a select few go in for the IIT Advanced. These details are there for all to know, and online exams also bring some more comfort to the students.

Madhav took exams in Mumbai, Mahati from Jalandhar at her grandparents' house, and finally Bhavin from Jaipur. Bhavin wanted to complete the whole process, give his best, and return to Mumbai. On the other hand, there was still some sort of silence between Swarna, Mahati's mother, and Mahati. In order to avoid this difficulty, it was a decision for Mahati to take exams at Jalandhar.

Though the physics paper was easy, the mathematics and chemistry papers were quite tough and mostly tested the basic understanding of the concepts in depth. In addition, the time for mathematics was much less, and only those students who had some natural talents could solve it.

All three cleared the IIT Mains and also wrote the IIT Advanced. The results were as expected, and many lost hope as the chemistry for many, which was generally very easy, finally worked out to be very tough.

Immediately after the exams are over, the coaching classes provide the model answer sheets, and you can evaluate your performance and the ranks you may expect for possible admission.

All three qualified, and Bhavin got the top 400 rank; Mahati got a rank above 1500; and Madhav got a very bad rank, and with that, that would not qualify him for admission at IITB, for the branch he has always wanted. Madhav always wanted to join Computer Sciences at IITB, and his dream to join IIT B ended there. Madhav decided to do computer engineering at NIT Surathkal, as he had visited it earlier and some of his own relatives stayed close to Udupi. Bhavin decided to do a dual degree (B.Tech. and M.Tech.) in Electrical Engineering, and that was possible with that rank. Mahati always wanted to join Aerospace Engineering at IITB, and she was the only one to get what she wanted.

It is important to mention that the difference in marks for many students may be a few marks, but there is a large change in the ranks. The computer takes the score and just adds it up and allots the ranks. In addition, it always remains for most of the students to get admission in computer, electrical, and mechanical, the most sought-after branches. Even after passing the toughest examination, these students who do not get their branch always feel bad, and this affects their studies. Many students who have worked very hard for 3 to 4 years, nonstop, feel a sense of burnout and lose interest in their studies. As the competition increases for a change of branch, this further puts pressure on it, and this unwanted competition creates stress that many students cannot handle. This leads to several aberrations, and before the parents could realise this, a few students got highly disturbed, leading to an emotional imbalance. A few IITs have decided to discontinue the change of branch to make the students comfortable at the chosen branch.

At this stage, it is important for parents and students to understand that this entire effort was worth the dividends the system can return. There is a need for parents to constantly evaluate their children before forcing them to take these exams. This needs introspection and evaluation: how has his son or daughter performed at X level, scholarship examinations, regional Olympiads, and finally NTSE, after feeling completely satisfied and, if needed, discussion with people who have gone through this rigour, make a conscious and informed decision. There may be many students who are just not meant for this exam, and there may be many who are not capable, so making a conscious decision in consultation with their teachers is a good idea. Finally, leave the decision to the student, and many drop out after paying the fees. There is a need for the utmost caution before jumping into this hard sea, which has many undercurrents that are never revealed at the surface. Even after getting admission, it is equally important to pass the course exams at IITs and maintain a decent balance between studies and extracurricular activities. This is easier said than done for many, and students drop semesters, leave the course altogether, and take up a different assignment. During this whole process, the student has lost precious years and ends up blaming himself for this ill-fated adventure. This is not to discourage students from appearing for this exam, but they should be mentally prepared to accept the realities. Just a pass or a fail at this examination does not evaluate the strength of any student.

Visit to IITB

Madhav quickly adjusted to the excellent campus at NIT Surathkal, and he was enjoying the excellent teaching provided by the faculty. There were a couple of phone calls from his friends at IITB and also once from Mahati, and Madhav personally rang Mahati and Bhavan for their excellent performances and congratulated them on their success at IITJEE and admission at the branches they always wanted to. Bhavin, as usual, was very happy that his dreams of Madhav were shattered, and he was also a bit upset not to get into the computer engineering branch. He was always scared that Madhav might do wonders as he got a hold of chemistry, and his commitment to physics, mathematics, and solving skills was excellent.

One of their common friends of Mahati from the same place from where Madhav comes informed Mahati that Madhav lost his mother just before the exams, and this shattered him and his performance was not at his best. Even with a few hours of study, he could clear but not get the rank to get admission to the branch of his choice.

Mahati immediately rang Bhavin and informed him about the tragedy of Madhav, and she said that during the holidays, they could travel together and say condolences together. Bhavin said he would send his condolence messages on WhatsApp and was not keen on accompanying Mahti and travelling all the way to Surathkal to meet Madhav. In addition, he has to attend a special course on computer architecture offered by the Computer Engineering Department. Mahati realised that Bhavin would not like to come, nor can she go, as this visit may not be approved by her family as she has to travel all alone.

The friendship between Bhavin and Mahati was growing in the absence of Madhav, but there was a strong pull towards Madhav at times, especially during the discussions she had at the temple.

As always said, out-of-site is out of mind, and with increasing demands on the academic side combined with the extracurricular activities, there was not much communication between all three.

It was during the third year that Madhav saw an announcement from IITB related to the "robotics competition - ROBOWARS" at IITB during the Techfest, an important event at IITB, and this institute was providing the necessary platform for displaying talents from various teams in India and abroad. This event was funded well by several industries, as the footfall during this event was very high.

Madhav had thought that this would be an opportunity to visit IITB and also meet his friends, as this provided a three-day stay at the IITB campus. In addition, he has taken many courses in robotics and also studied a few online courses offered by several universities in India and abroad. Madhav was fascinated, as this could be a learning experience, and he also showed his talent and sharpened his own skills.

Madhav met the HOD of the Computer Engineering Department and wanted to know more about this event. As he was busy, he asked a faculty member, Prof. Advaith Sharma, who joined the department recently after completing his Ph.D. from Cornel, US. He was an excellent teacher, good faculty, and was also a good mentor for many students. As Madhav was the topper of his branch, Prof. Sharma said that he would meet them all as a team on Saturday after 2 p.m. due to his own prior commitments. He just said building robots for a competition needs good skills from electrical and mechanical backgrounds students, as well as any students from computer hardware. In addition, they need funds to make this robot, which is at least closer to the last-year prototypes. The prize money and honour of winning are something big that made Madhav take a serious plunge.

Madhav had approached his close friend Mr. Radhakanth from the Mechanical Engineering Department, and he had shown exemplary skill in machine design. They approached Miss Anita, who is from the electrical engineering department; she joined NITS because of the palace and Brach; in fact, Anita would have gotten admitted to IITB, the mechanical engineering department. Her parents are from Udupi, and they admitted her to NITS. Now they were searching for a student from a computer hardware specialist, and the HOD suggested the name of Mr. Marsh from Germany, as he had come as an exchange student. In addition, Mr. March had a passion for seeing India and its vast culture. Within days, the team was ready, and they made a short presentation to impress Prof. Sharma about their seriousness. HOD had given a phone call and confirmed that a local manufacturer, Arun Swamy, had agreed to fund the entire expenditure for this project, and the only wish was that they should at least top 10 selected among 150 participants. Arun Swamy had seen this competition earlier at IITB and wanted to contribute as this would not cost him a big fortune. He had also narrated to the team how bitter and tough it becomes as they move up the ladder. This was very happy news for all four, and the HOD has written to the Tech Fest about NITS participation as there were not many other teams wishing to put in extra hard work apart from doing their regular studies.

Few people are born to work hard throughout their lives to get something substantial, and this gives them satisfaction. In fact, for Madhav, it has become an ambition, and he was willing to make any commitment to prove that he had the strength and vigour to excel. The happiness you derive when you beat an enemy who is apparently mightier than you is satisfaction for a lifetime. Madhav could not join IITB, with which he has struggled for three years, and his close friends have joined with nearly the same talent. In addition, beating someone in front of their home and deriving happiness cannot be underestimated. At that time, he remembered the thought given by his mother: do any activity with all resources at your command and leave the fruit to the Lord Siva, and this is the only way of giving the best. Sometimes these battles are not on the same front, and being from NITS, losing was not a big issue, but winning was big news, as this proves talent exists anywhere; you only have to nurture it.

Prof. Sharma was waiting for the two other students, Anita and Radhakanth, on a Saturday afternoon, and that was the time they met and discussed. Being a faculty member, Prof. Sharma was too busy to spare time. The two, Anita and Radhakanth, arrived two hours late and expressed a sincere apology as they had some unfinished assignments and time was running out.

To this end, Prof. Sharma narrated a story about commitment.

It was during the Second World War and near the Russian border, and due to heavy shelling by the enemy army, the Russians were losing their tanks and so were their soldiers. This loss was too much, and the general of the Russian army felt they needed better steel material for their tanks. If we do not have one, there is every chance of losing the war. In fact, they got some time due to the advancement of the cold, as this will require a tough time for enemy soldiers to adjust to the extremely unfavourable weather conditions.

The General visited a very reputed metallurgical lab involved in materials development in Russia and posed this problem to the scientists and engineers. The general also promised all help, both financially and in terms of manpower and equipment necessary for developments, rather quickly. No one was willing to take on such a huge responsibility, and all were looking at other faces. Finally, a young engineer about 30 years old said, Sir, I promise to deliver a high-quality steel material that will stand against enemy bullets. The general agreed and provided all the necessary help and said, "When should he return to collect that material for their use? The young engineer said, "Sir, in six months."

The general said, "Shall you come in forenoon or afternoon?"

This was shocking and surprising, and the young engineer and the urgency were very well underlined.

After exactly six months, the general arrived and asked for the material for testing by his own soldiers. The material was there, and the young engineer kept his word and delivered the material.

The general ordered, "Please bring all the relatives of these young engineers and keep the newly developed material as a shield and fire, assuming this is a battleground."

Around sixty of the relatives of the young engineer were brought, and the newly developed steel was kept in front of them as a shield and indiscriminate firing was done.

There was no need to go after that, and all survived. The moral of the story is to deliver what you promised.

This story was in the minds of all students, and they were never late to the project and learned the habit of delivering what they had promised throughout their lives.

They worked very hard for the next three months as a team, and this has taught all of them, especially Madhav and his team members, many important lessons and understandings in several areas that normally could not be done in the typical classroom study.

Madhav was good at using several aspects of artificial intelligence (AI), as he has done an online course and was willing to use some of these concepts and develop the robots for use during "robo-war." In addition, Madhav made a small robot that has a near-human face and reciprocates the emotions of any human standing in front of the robot. This has attracted many students and faculty at NITS, and he has single-handedly made this robot as it involved very complex algorithms and mathematical models and relatively little computer hardware. The special properties of this robot was its ability to express emotions, especially mimicking the person standing in front of it. In addition, it reads the emotions of the person, and if that person is angry or raises his voice, the robot expresses a blissful smile and changes the mood of that person. There are close to 20 emotions loaded in the system, and the robot never picks up the same emotion successively. This was a marvel, and all agreed that Madhav was a genius, and all appreciated Madhav.

In the meantime, with the help of Prof. Sharma and all his friends, made a robot that had a lethal weapon inside and looked very simple externally. It was displayed for all students and faculty to see, and appreciation started pouring in. All four students became best friends, and they gave their best for making the robot and worked very hard without sacrificing their studies.

The final day at IITB has arrived. There were close to 150 robots selected across India for the "Robo War." and there were several preliminary rounds. NITS-Robot did well, and none of the robots were even coming close to NITS-Robot. As soon as preliminary rounds were over, he just called Bhavin first and wanted to meet him. Bhavin was staying nearby and spent some time, and Bhavin's robot could not be qualified as there was a selection of robots from IITB and it did not come to a level that deserves to represent IITB. Bhavin felt a bit unhappy and did not say anything about this, but wished Madhav the best of luck for his team. When Madhav showed the second Robo, which showed emotions, Bhavin was just astonished at the hardware and software level to which Madhav elevated himself. That was too big, and he did not ask for more details and pretended as if he understood. It was Madhav's turn to speak to Mahati, and they together went to the Powai Lake and spoke for hours about their families, Mahati was quite happy about several things Madhav had done to her. It was nearly 4 a.m., and it was time to leave as the competition was to start at 9.30 a.m. Mahati just bunked her class to see the performance of the robots, and she was astonished to see NITS Robots, and they looked lethal. In addition, the robot, which showed emotions from NITS, was selected as a robot to greet the chief guest, the Honourable Chief Minister of Maharastra, and other guests. The emotions displayed by the robot were close and so attractive that the CM of Maharashtra announced a special prize for this robot and requested the organisers make a few and place them near the entrance assembly to invoke gentleness for all legislators before entering the assembly. This news came on the front page of all leading newspapers, and the footprint at the festival increased tenfold.

Several countries and leading manufacturers were there to look at the talent. NITS-Robo and the one from VJTI-Robo were there in the final, and more than 10,000 students were watching. Finally, it was no surprise that VJTI Robo won the competition, and NITS Robo was awarded as the next best contestant as a first-time entry. All the leading manufacturers were impressed by the Robo, which showed emotion. And they wanted to meet Madhav to know more about that, as that has the potential to be incorporated into their production line.

Finally, it was a joy; NITS Robo and VJTI were declared joint winners, and the event was covered by both national and international media. Madhav, along with his team, went to receive the award certificates, and the jury had a special word of appreciation for this robot, which showed emotions, CM was personally present to give away a special prize to Madhav.

That day was the most blissful and happy moment experienced by Madhav and his team. During the final round, Vishnu, Madhav's father, was present, and he very much appreciated Madhav and his team members. He has invited them all to a dinner at his residence. A special invitation was also extended to Bhavin and Mahati. Bhavin could not attend that dinner; however, Mahati attended. Mahati was surprised to see Vishnu, who has so much grace and maturity, and the understanding between son and father was there to see, and their coordination was at its best. Mahati could also witness the middle-class house and felt that this is where human values are born and remain throughout their lives.

As the team returned to NITS, there was Prof. Sharma at the station along with a few students to receive the victorious team. Very few times in life, happiness also does not die down very fast, and it must sink in very slowly.

The next day, there was an email from a leading Robo manufacturer appreciating NITS Robo and extending an invitation to visit the USA for a presentation on the Robo, which displayed emotions that impressed many. It was during that trip that Madhav felt the rewards of hard work, and Mahati was there to see him off at Mumbai airport. Mahati unknowingly began to develop feelings for Madhav, which had been quite dormant, and Madhav never expressed it explicitly.

Before Madhav's planned visit to the USA, he had written to leading universities, especially those where the best possible supercomputers exist.

He received positive replies from a few, and many promised to provide him with local travel and hospitality. Madhav wanted to spend three months in the US if he obtained an internship fellowship. This was just the beginning, with many more visits to follow soon.

Madhav's Maiden Visit to the USA

Madhav took a round-trip flight to save some money so that he could spend it locally, and he was flying to New York, a city that never sleeps and has an infrastructure that has matured and leaves many cities, especially infrastructures, behind in different countries.

Madhav was always read many times in "Target IIT and Destination US" by many of his own seniors and also in the leading newspapers. Recently, he has also heard that "if you open the flood gates of the US, half of the Indian population may migrate to the US; and finally, the US is a land of opportunities, where there is a work culture and, above all, an echo system that exists for many to give their best. The US has more than three times the area of India, and on the other hand, the US population is just 1/3 of the population of India. GDP per capita in India is less than $2,000, and in the US it is about $70,000. It has a large number of the best universities in the world. Needless to say, the US has better infrastructure and also attracts the best talent across the world, especially from Asian countries, India and China. This is the place that naturally leads to the best echo systems for innovation. In addition, people work their best, and the individual work is respected and paid as per their capabilities. There may be pay parity across genders, though this discrimination was seen at times in higher positions. No wonder so many Indians wanted to settle down in the US because of the high quality of life. Approximately, around fifty lakh Indians might be in the US; many more may be migrants; and many Indian Americans have occupied very high positions in the US. The average salary of Indians is higher than that of the average American working class. The flip side of Indians staying in the US is known to all, and there is no need to further stress it at this stage.

Madhav had made several attempts before his departure to the USA to understand the phenomenal growth of the USA and why it has become the number one destination country in the world, where all talented people like to move and settle, especially Indians and Chinese. Madhav always wanted to understand the reasons for the growth of the USA, which became the world's leading industrial power at the turn of the 20th century. This is not an easy question to understand, and many wanted to leave their own country due to their own personal ambitions and needs. It was an individual choice, and the USA attracts and allows talented people to settle down and contribute to their economy.

The flight landed a bit late in the evening, and many warned him to stay at the airport for safety and travel the next day. He could take local transportation in the early morning to his hotel. As this was his first maiden flight, he was a bit scared looking at the massive airport and the transport facilities that exist 24x7. No one came from the industry side to pick him up at the airport, and he just called the host and said he had reached his hotel. The host said he will pick him up in the morning at 9.00 am, and he can take up the BF and wait for him. Contrary to the treatment, he got in the USA, Madhav, went to Mangalore airport to pick up foreign guests to NITS, and this was his first time visiting the US, and the company could have sent someone to help him reach the hotel. He could sense the difference. If any foreign dignitary is visiting us in India, he is doing us a favour, and if you are visiting them, they are doing us a favor. Little did Madhav know that the facilities are excellent in many advanced nations, contrary to what we have in India. This fact is not easy for many Indians to understand and assimilate.

Madhav reached the hotel as early as 7 a.m., was ready by about 8.30, and was waiting for Mr. John to pick him up.

There were a couple of presentations from the company people about their products, and now it was the turn of Madhav to make his presentation about his robot, which used AI for showing emotions. Prof. Sharma went through the presentation of Madhav, and he made several suggestions, and it lasted about an hour. The art of any presentation to get better attention from the audience and also get appreciation was to make a presentation in such a manner that only 20% of the material is understood and the rest, 80%, goes overboard for the audience. and

Prof. Sharma from NITS has perfected this art, and he has transferred to Madhav. Madhav's presentation was well received and appreciated, and they have offered him a pre-placement offer to join this company as soon as he completes his B.Tech. degree, and they have also promised an attractive salary package. There were a couple of questions during the presentation, and Madhav explained and answered all the questions satisfactorily. Madhav was overwhelmed with joy about his placement offer at the end of his third year, which many students dream to get.

The host took him on a guided tour, and Madhav could see for himself the city and nearby places, and many times he was making a mental comparison of cities in India, Kota, Surathkal, and Mumbai, a few places he was familiar with.

Madhav then moved to a few universities and made some more presentations, and all were well appreciated. He had learned a lot during the questions and interactions, and during these interactions, he could access how little he knew and identify his gap areas. The top university has offered an intern during the summer for three months, which included local hospitality, boarding and lodging, the facilities at the university, and the necessary supervision for his project. Now, Madhav has to find finances for his trip to the USA. Madhav has decided to ask his father, the only source for him to find his travel. Such a wealthy nation with so many funds could not understand why they were not paying for his travels as well.

A few of his Indian friends, who stayed there for a few years, said, "Learn about the American system; this is a materialistic and capitalistic society, and only the fittest will survive." There is no humanity, and the system is not as liberal as in India. Everything appears good externally, but as you take a deep dive, you know what this system is all about.

One of his Indian American friends at one of the top universities for an intern explained the concept of "start-end-accelerator syndrome." Madhav said he is not aware of SAES, and his friend said not many Indian Americans may also know. This is the day you land up in the

American system, you press your accelerator of performance, like in a plane after taking off from a runway, and now you cannot reduce the speed or accelerator of performance with age, and the day you try to reduce, there is every chance that you will be weeded out of the system, likely to be replaced with someone equally capable with a reduced salary. In addition, the system allows you to perform at your best, and generally talent is appreciated and paid for, but they may not allow your parents to settle down. This means the system believes only in investing in you and trying their best to get the maximum; however, your parents have to stay in India, and they may not be allowed to settle along with you. Now, you know what the flip side of US quality of life is. They kept on discussing the pros and cons of the US vs. India. It is not that many who have settled in the US are quite happy, and they have their own problems that the American system throws at times.

Many Indians settled in America are in the service, administrative, hospitality, and business sectors. They are doing a great job, and there is no doubt they are paid well. If you are in the high-end R&D sector, working in the front-end areas of science and technology, the echo system in the US cannot be replaced in India, and there is every reason to continue in the US as this activity to get it done in India is not easy. Finally, another friend who is well settled in the US said that if you stay in the US for more than 5 years, rehabilitating in India is not an easy option. In this case, Madhav, if you can get a decent job at a place in India where your parents stay and have accommodation and are not interested in high-end R&D jobs, the quality of life you get in India is equal to or much better in the USA. This information had a strong influence on Madhav's mind. Madhav wanted to provide a high-end R&D culture in India that is close to what is available in the US while at the same time being close to parents.

Madhav made up his mind that he would visit the US to learn and establish contacts and may never settle in the US, and Madhav always thought of his father, Vishnu, who needs him with time. His father means everything to him, and taking care of him at an advanced age was his passion and not just an activity. His decision at that age was good or wrong; only time will tell.

Madhav had an excellent experience and learned many things in the US during his short trip. Mahdav visited the US again during the summer holidays at that university, which offered him an internship and provided an opportunity to use supercomputing for his AI and modelling work. During his stay for three months, he could write a report, which was subsequently published in a leading journal. This small work was very much appreciated by his supervisor and by other researchers working in this area.

Madhav returned to India after spending three months in the US, and this short stay gave him future directions for his career in India. During his stay, he made a few friends who had their own design centres and were also looking to offload some of their work in India, as this involved the complexity of using computers and mathematics for applying AI to real-time problems. In addition, Madhav had opportunities to learn and interact so that he could continue this work in India.

Madhav, on his return from the US, stayed at IITB Hostels with Bhavin's friend, who was on vacation. Bhavin could not get an internship in the US but spent some time doing an internship in Germany and had opportunities to travel extensively in Europe. However, Mahati chose to stay back in India and travelled along with his parents and brother to Singapore. The course for her at IITB was demanding, so she decided to relax and spend some quality time with her parents. This has helped to smooth the relationship with her mother. However, her mother was not quite happy with the carrier option taken by Mahati.

Madhav visited Mahati's Place for a few hours on the way to the airport. Mahati's father recognised Madhav and recollected with fond memories about his help to Mahati when she was admitted to a hospital in Kota. However, Mahati's mother failed to recognise Madhav, and no one knows whether she pretended not to recognise him or whether she has actually not recognised him. Mahati was quite upset with the treatment given to Madhav during a short stay of less than a few hours. Madhav could also understand the undercurrent at Mahati's House. He could see that Mahati's father was a bit incoherent, his hands were shaking, and he appeared to be in some sort of pain or discomfort. He has tried his best to concede this, and at times it was quite visible. Mahati and Madhav shared many of their experiences, and especially Madhav shared his learning experience in the US.

The Carrier Path of Madhav

Madhav did exceedingly well at B.Tech at NITS and was awarded the best student performance award, a gold medal, and a citation. During the convocation, Vishnu was present. Madhav very much missed his mother and felt her absence.

Madhav had many friends who had supported him during his stay at Surathkal, and this bond blossomed with time. They visited many nearby historical places and had many treks, and visits to Udupi temple were important for Madhav during the weekends. Many of his friends had so much fun and shared their best and worst times at NITS, and these are treasures most of the students cherished, and these memories become more intense with time. These were and will be golden moments in any student's life.

Madhav always kept in touch with all his professors at NITS especially Prof. Sharma, who had helped them during the project. The team that had made the ROBO joined again to make a small ROBO for the department from the funds Madhav saved during his short stay as an intern in the US. This gift was very much appreciated by all the faculty, especially Prof. Sharma. Prof. Sharma advised him to continue his studies and advised him to join MS leading to a Ph.D. at IISc at Bengalure. Madhav also kept in touch with Arun Samy (who funded their robot activity).

Madhav had cleared his GATE exam and joined ME leading to his Ph.D. at IISc in Bangalore, and his learning at that institute, especially the basic concepts, were really stepping stones for his entrepreneurial activities in the future.

Mahati decided to move to Cornell University in the US to do an MS leading to a Ph.D. programme, and Bhavin also joined the prestigious MIT for his MS programme and later did his MBA from Stanford.

Both the parents of Mahati and Bhavin were not happy about their going to the US. Mahati's mother pleaded with her to do an MBA in hospital management in the US, but Mahati refused. Against the wishes of her parents, Mahati moved to the US to pursue her Ph.D. programme. When Mahati's mother threatened that they did not have enough funds to support education for studies in the US, Mahati took an education loan and also received some financial waivers from the university and took up some jobs in the US to make ends meet. Later, Mahati did not accept any financial support from her parents. Both parents and children might make mistakes out of anger, and both should be accommodating and forgiving. This is the main mantra for a good relationship.

Bhavin's parents wanted Bhavin to settle down in India and take up the family business. There was a hunger protest from Bhavin's mother and also a threat not to accept Bhavin when he returned. Nothing could stop Bhavin from proceeding to the US. It is difficult to comment on the nature of a few individuals, and they can become very unreceptive and demanding, and very hard on themselves. This will not help either party. There is a need to convince children by the parents through love and affection, and if nothing works, allow them to let go and accept the final decision of the children.

Vishnu never interfered with Madhav's academic programmes and allowed him to make informed and mature decisions. What works like magic is the upbringing, and there is a need for parents to be role models for their children, instead of being only harsh and demanding. Vishnu had no expectations, and he had only advised Madhav to do what he liked, and he is free to take up any assignment either in India or abroad.

Preparation for IITJEE made them very tolerant of hardships; failures made them mentally tough, and determination made them achieve impossible targets to achieve the end results in their favour.

Madhav always wanted to be an entrepreneur and wanted to have his own consultancy and manufacturing facility in Bangalore and live his life on his terms. He never felt the need to take up a job and do what others wanted; he wanted to do something different on his terms. He wanted that freedom. Immediately after completing his Ph.D., Madhav got funding, initially from a small consultancy unit, and then started getting orders from his friends in the US and also from Japan. Madhav had seen many failures in the beginning, but after several trips to the US, he secured funding and he had made a huge capital, and started his own firm, making a name and fame for himself. Many leading industrialists and manufacturers wanted to cooperate with Madhav, and after initial problems, there was no limit to his success, and his company became the leading company in the world in the areas of using AI Predictive modelling, Reliability, data analytics, virtual realities, blockchains, 5G network, and automation.

In addition, Madhav was a mastermind, and he had mentored several companies that were making robots for export. He had his own shares and consultations, and these companies survived international competition based on in-house innovation, which was essential, Madhav could provide these details to the manufacturers in India for them to survive. No one doubted the capabilities of Madhav, and this kept manufacturers grounded, and they also depended on the necessary inputs from Madhav. There were always cordial relationships between the selected companies and Madhav, and Madhav was never demanding; he wanted Indian companies to survive in the international market. Madhav always remembered the financial help provided by Arun Swamy during his NITS days, and he also made him a partner in one of his firms, which helped Arun Swamy grow exponentially.

Madhav continued to stay with his father in Bangalore and helped him wherever it was necessary, keeping his promise to stay with his father. At no stage of his life did he ever even think of leaving his country. This commitment made him who he is and also kept him on his toes to be very innovative to sustain international competition. His company received the award for the best entrepreneur of that year, and his products reached worldwide.

Bhavin Meeting Mahati at Cornell

Bhavin, after completing his MBA programme at Stanford, accepted a position at a leading American bank. He was quite happy about his success. He had everything he wanted and could visit India at his will to meet his parents. He was content with his success. As time progressed, his workload increased, and demands from the management became too much, taking a heavy toll on him. He kept in touch with Mahati, who, after completing her Ph.D., was looking for a postdoc position and was trying her best.

Bhavin had always had a soft spot for Mahati. He was well-placed, but due to his attitude towards his colleagues, he had a few issues and had made attempts to change his attitude.

Bhavin decided to travel by car to Cornell to meet Mahati. After reaching Cornell, Bhavin said he was there for some assignment and requested some time to meet that evening, to which Mahati readily agreed.

They meet at a hotel, and after initial pleasantries, Bhavin initiates a heart-touching conversation with Mahati.

Mahati, just look, we are good friends and have kept in constant touch for more than 10 years since I met in Kota.

"I feel like I am now earning well in the US and am also planning to settle down in the US, and I might get green card status at any time. I genuinely like you, and I also feel you like me, and I agree that you have never expressed that to me explicatively.

I know both of our families are comfortable with taking our relationships further, and I will assure you a good life. I will also promise you that I will give you my best. In addition, I now have an MBA from Standford, and I have a bright future. At present, I am looking for companionship and have been attracted to it from the beginning.

Please tell me your opinion, and I will request that my father speak to your parents in Mumbai.

Mahati just kept quiet and did not utter a word.

Bhavin, I am not keen on settling in the US and want to get back to India and start a fresh life. Money was never a criteria for me in a relationship, and I do not think we are compatible. Please forgive me if I am very harsh.

At this stage, Bhavin gets very angry.

I knew you were attracted to Madhav, and a person even could not pass an IITJEE, and all of us made our efforts to teach him. Madhva does not even have a job, and he is not only adamant but also highly selfish. This is my personal, frank opinion about Madhav.

"Bhavin!" shouted Mahati.

"Please do not force your opinion and your thoughts into my mouth, and the relationship between us is more of a personal choice. As far as money is concerned, I have to just go back to India and accept the work given by my parents. Be assured, I have so much money that I can never earn in the US by staying for another 30 years. I had a passion to do studies, and please understand. I know you do not like Madhav, and that is your personal choice. Please never criticise Madhav in front of me."

"Just tell me a single quality that Madhav had in him that is better than mine; even though he has no good sense of humour or a decent quality of life, he has no character to boast about himself". Bhavin said loudly.

Mahati just kept silent and allowed Bhavin to pour all his emotions against Madhav.

Mahati said, "If you say that Madhav does not have character, than none of us do. Madhav is a good human being, courageous, and above all, genuinely concerned about me. He kept in touch with me at all occasions. Madhav always worked for my relationship with my parents and also took care of me when I was at the hospital. Madhav had no self-interest, and even he does not know how rich my parents are. I am not sure if he likes me, and he has never expressed his feelings towards me. I think I will be very safe with Madhav, and I do not know how to handle it if he rejects me. Finally, I would like to add that Madhav is different and humble, and I just fell in love with him without knowing that I had fallen in love. This has not happened to you. Yes, he is not from IIT and may not have a good job, but surely he will get one.

Bhavin, we are good friends, and inherently, you know about yourself, and you also have great admiration for Madhav. Let us stop this further and let us part ways. I wish you all the best." Saying this, Mahati left the hotel, leaving Bhavin lost for hours.

This was their last meeting in the US.

After that, Bhavin made a few more attempts to get closer to Mahati but was not always successful. However, he kept in touch with Mahati.

Bhavin meeting Madhav in India

At times, Mahati was getting frustrated and felt that she should have taken up an MBA in hospital management and returned to India to be with her parents. Additionally, Mahati had her own problems with her supervisor during the Ph.D. programme, as he had very high expectations for Mahati, and she was not able to meet these requirements. As many would expect, a Ph.D. is the highest degree and demands a lot from students, making it very hard for many students to complete in a meaningful time. In any case, with all her strength, Mahati managed to finish her Ph.D. programme and finally secured a postdoc position at another prestigious university based on quality publications and an improved Curriculum Vitae (CV). During that time, Bhavin met her a couple of times and tried his best to enhance their friendship. Bhavin was convinced that Mahati had a fascination towards Madhav, which she never could express, either at Kota or later after moving to the US. In fact, there was not much communication between them. Both of them knew that Madhav had decided to stay back in India and had taken a path that he liked. However, they never knew that Madhav had completed his Ph.D. in record time and was known for his work in the field of AI and other related areas.

Madhav, with all his contributions to the company, was chosen as the Managing Director of that company by investors. He never behaved like an MD and believed in community living, treating everyone equally. This approach bonded him with many. This rapport with his colleagues was essential to contribute intensively. In fact, none of the employees left the company, as they had a decent salary, company shares, and, above all, quality work leading to intellectual and job satisfaction. Madhav was fairly successful in bringing the right kind of work culture, equivalent to that in the US, or at times even better, all while being in close proximity to his father.

One afternoon, when Madhav was deeply involved in analysing a specific problem related to AI for use in repetitive thinking patterns of the human mind, a colleague brought in an email from a leading American bank requesting the use of AI for data analytics to understand the spending patterns of its customers using credit cards. This was an area they had never thought about before. The email also stated that Mr. Bhavin from Washington, DC, would like to visit and discuss with the company's engineers, as their bank was keen on using the tools to be developed. This was possibly the first of its kind to use these tools to understand the spending behaviour of the elite class.

Madhav did not read the content but focused his attention on Bhavin, the visitor. Immediately, Madhav advised his friend to accept Bhavin's visit to his company and also specially requested his HR department take care of the visitor right from receiving him at the airport and also provide the accommodation at the company expense. Generally, this company was visited by many, but Madhav never asked HR to take care of it, and as a general policy, the company never supported facilitating the logistics in Bangalore. Not many times did Madhav meet the visitors, and there were several layers before meeting MD, and this meeting was arranged only if necessary. This was big news for his colleagues that Madhav has shown special concern to Bhavin and relaxed this rule that is also coming from the banking industry.

Bhavin was surprised to receive excellent hospitality at Bangalore airport from a company relatively unknown to him "AI-Mapping." He never bothered to know the details of the company, and he thought that it was a routine business as usual, and some Indian companies wanted some work from the US to make some money. Somewhere, Bhavin was thinking, How come his bank has selected some obscure company, "AI-Mapping." for solving some of the complex problems of a leading American bank? Arrogance of this sort is not totally unexpected, and this is experienced by many Indian companies.

Bhavin was astonished to see Madhav standing at the portago, and Madhav personally opened the car door to welcome Bhavin. This was disgusting to the HR department, and never was MD there to receive a foreign guest. This does not mean guests were not respected, but were given all importance, just as any Indian receives when they visit the US. This was the norm of "AI-Mapping." and this norm was broken for the first time.

Bhavin, for the moment, thought that Madhav was an employee and, on the advice of his HR department, was facilitating his visit to "AI-Mapping."

Madhav hugged Bhavin in front of his HR people, and Bhavin was equally at ease, and it appeared to many in HR that they knew each other well before and no one had any idea of the struggle they had at Kota. There was no need to explain all the facts and keep all guessing, which brings in fun and much attention.

Bhavin was astonished at the huge complex of more than ten floors, much better than the many buildings near by. He was astonished at the architectural design, and Madhav explained the significance of the idea behind the shape and size of the company. After initially presentations by many departments and finally by HR, Madhav had personally taken to other units and introduced to many directors, and some of these areas had futuristic concepts. Bhavin was surprised that everyone in the company was addressing him as sir with respect, including the Head of Data Analytics. There was a suspension in his mind, and he was not mentally prepared to accept that. That is what is yet to evolve.

Finally, Bhavin saw, which he had never thought of seeing, the name plate "Madhav, Managing Director."

Bhavin's worst dreams have come true, and the earth beneath his feet is sinking. He blamed himself for not studying about "AI mapping" before coming to visit. If he had known, Bhavin had all the resources to send someone else, as there are many Indians and they are keen on visiting India as they can combine their personal visits. Madhav took him inside and was happy to receive him. He explained and interacted with Bhavin in person for about 2 hours and explained the success story of the AI mapping."

Bhavin never in life was humble, and Bhavin for the first time realised that Madhva would make it big and no one could contain a talent, and it was no surprise that his bank has elected "AI-Mapping" for this work. There is a need for his bank to work with AI mapping and not the other way. Bhavin went a bit blank several times during informal talks with Madhav, and finally he came to terms with reality.

All and every moment at Kota was there in front of him and how unkind he was, and in spite of all this, Madhav never was against him, always humble and never was threatening, but only he himself was feeling a bit inferior, a dwarf in front of Madhav. Bhavin then also knew it was his talent and passion for the work, not just his degree or the institute from which he received it. Institutes are always bigger than individuals. Bhavin became normal, and Bhavin shifted his attention to his personal life and said that he was married to a Chinese girl due to several circumstances, and he had his own ups and downs in life. He also said Patels was quite unhappy about his marriage and never approved, and he is struggling to come to terms. He said a few things just happen and they are beyond any body control. He thought of returning to India and being with his parents, but it was not easy with his family. Madhav immediately congratulated Bhavin, wished him well, and said he would meet his wife a bit later in the evening. In fact, that day night, all of them had a good party in a hotel near the place of his company. Madhav's company was liked by Bhavin's wife, and Madhav had no inhibitions about that girl.

Madhav said that it took some time to build his company and that he was just following the advice of his father. There was sometimes long silence and sometimes so much warmth between them, and Madhav has advised his HR not to send phone calls during his informal talks with Bhavin.

In the end, just before departure, Bhavin said, "Mahati has returned from the US and has taken a position at IISc, and she has on several occasions expressed her love towards you, Madhav." Bhavin also said that it was indeed a fact that he liked Mahati; "However, she said on several occasions that she treated him as her best friend and that there were no further strings attached to this relationship. She also said to me that on several occasions she wanted to express her love to you, Madhav, but could not. Mahati could not understand what was on your mind, Madhav. Please speak to her, take this journey to a different level, and give it the destination it deserves." Now, it was the turn of Madhav to get surprised by his attitude towards Mahati, and he could not read her mind. Maybe he is not good at it, and at times Madhav felt bad as he could not understand Mahati's mind. Madhav did his best to conceal his emotions; however, Bhavin could read the changing colours of Madhav and what he was thinking too deeply.

Before leaving, Bhavin said he would be in touch and his company would be happy to work with AI mapping, and Madhav came all the way down to see Bhavin. Bhavin felt a bit heavy before leaving Madhav; both became a bit emotional. On his return to the hotel, Bhavin felt a bit light after receiving so much love and hospitality and a feeling of goodwill, a feeling he had never experienced during his stay in the US for more than 10 years, and that too came from a friend with whom he was always envious.

Chapter IV

Destiny

This world is not perfect nor are the people living in it.

Accepting people who matter to you wholeheartedly with all their differences, inadequacies and insensitivities is absolutely essential to live blissfully.

The Right Direction

It was early morning with a very cold breeze welcoming the passengers at Bangalore International Airport.

Mahati was waiting in the lounge to fly to Hyderabad to deliver her invited talk at an Internal Conference at a leading educational institute. She was busy scanning through the PowerPoint presentations and making corrections.

Just then, Madhav came and sat very close beside Mahati and greeted her with an affectionate smile and a gentle touch. Mahati felt surprised, looking for something familiar, but internally, she could feel the warmth of that touch.

Mahati said, "I'm flying to Hyderabad for a presentation."

Madhav replied, "I'm flying to Delhi for an important meeting with defence scientists."

Madhav knew that Bhavin must have briefed Mahati about his interaction at "AI mapping."

There were exchanges of pleasantries, but mostly there was a loss of words and silence. Silence conveys emotions when words fail.

Madhav asked Mahati for her boarding pass and then walked away to connect with his HR.

After a couple of minutes, the organisers accepted Mahati's request for an online presentation of her invited speech. She was stunned to see a letter from the organisers, and she knew that Madhav must have been behind it. It was a wonder, and she chose to keep silent as Mahati never liked someone else interfering with her freedom.

We grant the freedom to be walked over only to those people whom we love intensely.

Madhav reached out for Mahati's hand, and she followed without a word. Both of them proceeded to gate number 11 from where private hired jets took off.

To her great surprise, the plane staff greeted Mahati and Madhav, and it appeared to Mahati that they knew Madhav well.

In a few minutes, the flight took off from Bangalore to unknown destinations in India. Neither Madhav nor Mahati bothered to inquire where they were heading.

Madhav extended his hand to Mahati, and time stood still.

The End

Epilogue

Happiness is transient, do not pursue it, and it might come when you are not guarded, just treasure it.

I was detached from that incident of my return from Kota and my short association with the Snehal's family and forgot this whole episode till that time, when I reinvented myself. Days, months, and years have passed, and time has made me forget many things.

I have to tell the readers to remember that incident when I met Snehal again after a gap of ten years. Most of the time, it is said that a few incidents may fade out momentarily but will be fresh when they reappear. I will tell you how.

It is not always that a research scientist from a government establishment is sent to the USA to present a paper at a conference. I know well that science, engineering, and innovation may be done in many countries, but the quantum leap in any field of science and engineering is largely done in the USA. I had the opportunity to visit many European countries, but never the USA. This was my first trip to the USA to attend a conference in Orlando, and I was quite happy that I had both finance and support from both the Indian government and the organiser of the conference in the US. Small things make people happy, and I was immensely pleased and looking forward to my first trip to the USA.

I had a pleasant trip to the US and must admit that my presentation in Orlando, USA, was well appreciated by several members of the international audience. It is important to mention two things that make individuals happy: sufficient money (not too much) and appreciation from established international delegates.

As I was enjoying that movement of momentary happiness at being appreciated, I felt a sensation at my feet as if someone were touching my feet.

A woman in her late 20s or early 30s with a small child was touching my feet, possibly for my blessing. I was taken aback, as I was not expecting this to happen that way in the USA. I just lifted her with both my hands and could see tears rolling down profusely. She was Snehal, more beautiful than I had seen her ten years ago, and possibly more mature. She informed me that she was chairing one of the sessions of this conference, and a very select few have this rare distinction; those have a very high level of accomplishment. Her eyes expressed happiness to see me, and this emotion cannot be expressed in words and should only be felt. She just touched my hands softly and introduced me to her husband and son; there was nothing more to add. I was just choked with emotions touched by love, affection, and warmth. I just could not control my emotions; tears rolled down my eyes.

Finally, to conclude, all of us have our own talents, both inborn and acquired with effort. There is a need to identify the talents to set goals that are achievable. No one can acquire or crave the talents of others. Have you ever seen an orchestra where everyone is performing rhythmically and in tune, and this effort transports you to another world? Have you ever seen a painter who uses his brush and paint on canvas with rhythm and dexterity to focus the mind? This painting takes you emotionally to places you have never been. Have you seen a writer who uses his pen to play with words and sentences and brings in emotions and joy or sorrow to his thoughts? Have you seen a scientist who works with a single-minded devotion to finding solutions to unresolved issues with nature? Have you ever seen a sportsman who utilises all his physical and mental energies to achieve the impossible? Have you ever seen a surgeon perform a complex operation with all his dexterity to revive life? These are all the pinnacles of excellence, where ambitions, aspirations, and talents coexist to bring out the best and achieve the impossible. These are all examples of pushing one's endurance limit to the extreme to achieve the impossible.

Finally, it is the mandate of individuals to identify their talents, which all of us have in abundance, and excel in our areas of knowledge and expertise.

www.ingramcontent.com/pod-product-compliance
Lightning Source LLC
LaVergne TN
LVHW091053150826
845673LV00002B/570